To: Professor David Jo

A memento of historical happenings at the Castle

With best wishes

Elizabeth Frisbee

FARNHAM CASTLE 2001
Board Member then Advisory Council

THE ANCIENT VENISON FEAST OF FARNHAM

by

F.W.CULVER

© F.W. Culver

All rights reserved

No part of this publication may be reproduced, stored in a retrieval system, or transmitted, in any form or by any means, electronic, mechanical, photocopying, recording or otherwise, without the prior permission of the copyright owner.

ISBN 0 9535897 0 6

A ClP catalogue record for this book is obtainable from the British Library.

Typeset and printed by West Somerset Free Press,
5 Long Street, Williton, Taunton, Somerset TA4 4QN.

Published by the author

The moral right of the author has been asserted.

Obtainable from the author or all good bookshops.

DISCLAIMER

Every possible effort has been made to contact copyright holders of photographs reproduced in this work. The author can entertain no claim from any person after publication.

THE ANCIENT VENISON FEAST OF FARNHAM

by

F.W.CULVER

*" No town was the worse for having a tradition
that kept it together."*
- St. John Brodrick.

Contents

Prologue	4
The Bishops' Charters 688-1566	5-10
Bailiffs and Burgesses 1566-1789	11-29
The Vestry 1789-1866	30-46
The Local Board 1866-1894	47-56
Farnham Urban District Council 1895-1974	57-85
The Farnham Consultative Committee 1974-1984	86-89
Farnham (Parish) Town Council 1984-	90-96
Epilogue	97
Bishop Brownlow North	98
The Close Seasons	99
The Venison Dinner Committee	100
Bibliography and Acknowledgements	101-102
Index	103-110

Prologue

Within the magnificent Great Hall of Farnham's 12th century Castle, the scene is set. The 155 guests engage in animated conversation; old friendships renewed, new friendships made. The men immaculate in their dinner jackets are more than matched by the ladies in their fine dresses. The flower bedecked tables lit by silver candelabra are overlooked by portraits of bygone Bishops of Winchester, and the ornately carved 17th century balustrade of the Minstrels Gallery.

The Master of Ceremonies, resplendent in his red-tailed coat, wing collar and white gloves, interrupts to announce the arrival of the venison. Conversation dries, spontaneous applause erupts; the chef enters with the haunch of venison and approaches the top table, for the first slice to be cut by a civic dignatory. A choice five course meal follows, and they settle down to be regaled, amused and informed by speeches honouring the Church and the Town. In this manner the time-honoured tradition of the annual Venison Dinner is observed for another year, although the setting has changed dramatically from that of 1605 when the bailiffs and burgesses of the Corporation first resolved to hold an annual Town Feast. The early feasts were held at the Goats Head and six other public houses in the town. In those days with the linen trade in decline, Farnham had become the hub of the corn trade in central southern England. The Lord of the Manor was the Bishop of Winchester, who occupied Farnham Castle, and whose deer herd was to provide a welcome supply of venison for the annual feast for over 300 years.

As the corn trade diminished, the burgeoning hop trade flourished, until the town became a virtual 'sea of hops'.

Following the bankruptcy of the Corporation, when the estates were returned to the See, and the imposition of a Hop Duty, the dinners soon became 'hop betting'; a unique occasion supported by the hop growers, brewers, and traders of the town. The hop industry reached its zenith during the early nineteenth century, but gradually declined in the face of fierce competition from Kent, and the conversion of the hop grounds to other uses.

The 20th century heralded further changes. Most significantly was a change in the boundary of the diocese which resulted in the formation of the new diocese of Guildford, with the inclusion of Farnham. Thus the link with the Bishop of Winchester was broken. Following the dispersal of the deer herd, the Bishop had vacated the Castle which remained in the possession of the Ecclesiastical Commissioners, but is today occupied by the Centre for International Briefing.

May this remaining relic of the liberality of "Good Olde Tymes" never cease.

The Bishops' Charters - 688 to 1566

The history of the Venison Dinner spans four centuries of Farnham's religious, commercial, economic, social and political change. It has formed a continuous and visible thread, drawing together the strong connection between the church and the people of Farnham, while simultaneously exposing the gradual erosion of the powers of the Bishops, the dramatic changes in trade, and the transfer of community duties from ecclesiastical bodies to secular authorities, with the consequent growth of political power.

The introduction of venison into the Bailiffs' feasts began during the occupation of Farnham Castle by the Bishops of Winchester as Lords of the Manor, and the management of the secular affairs of the town by a Corporation comprising two Bailiffs and twelve Burgesses.

In order to understand how the decision to hold a Farnham Town Feast originated, it is necessary to peruse the various Charters which resulted in the creation of a Corporation. These Charters were not Royal Charters, therefore certain rights, notably the power to impose the death penalty, were withheld. The earliest Charter extant was the granting of Farnham to Bishop Wilfred by King Caedwalla in 688, apparently for the purpose of building a monastery. The Charter contains a warning: "But if by arrogant invasion presume by tyranny to infringe or diminish this gift made by me let him be severed from all christian society, but the gift remains none the less in its strength."

Thus began the relationship of Farnham with the Bishops. From the King a gift to religion. Such gifts by a monarch were said to provide comfort, and secure the benevolence of God, when, as was the custom in feudal times, the monarch was abroad engaged in the Crusades. There is no evidence of the monastery having been built. The Charter of 839 followed. This required the provision of two nights lodgings for the Bishop every year on his journey from Winchester to London. The Castle had yet to be built, so it suggests that other suitable accommodation was thought to be available.

The Charter of 858 mentions the 60 hides of Farnham sufficient for the needs of its population at that time, (one hide being sufficient to support one family). The Charter is in two sections and asserts the authority of the Bishop.

(1) The Bishop of St Swithuns grants the land to Aethelbond, King of West Saxona.

(2) The King directs that, after his departure from life "the same land shall revert to the Bishop and all the congregation of the Church of Winchester". In return this gift to the Bishop, the King returns it with greater value.

He declares that "the land shall be free, for ever, from all royal services except what we know as the "Trinada Necessitas," the threefold obligation.

(1) To render military services to the King in wartime

(2) To keep all bridges in repair.

(3) To fortify strongholds.

The second of these obligations, re-enacted under a local agreement in respect of the bridges at Tilford, was to prove too onerous to the Bailiffs and Burgesses in the later part of the seventeenth century, and result in a humiliating forfeiture to the Bishop of the title and rights of the Corporation.

The fourth Charter of 909 confirms the estates of Farnham to the Bishops of Winchester. It is bi-lingual - part latin, part anglo saxon.

During the period to the next Charter of 1248, it is noteworthy that the Bishop of Winchester had the management of the town at his disposal. He received all tolls, held fairs and markets, and in fact, was the feudal landlord of Farnham and the surrounding country. Fairs and markets were in these times very lucrative, and the power to hold them was granted as an especial privilege by the King himself. Originally on a Sunday, the fair was changed to a Thursday by a writ dated the 7th year of the reign of King John. There were Bailiffs at this time, and it is possible that Farnham was described as a Borough. It is suggested in the British Book of Charters that this occurred sometime between 1042 and 1660. No confirmation exists, as a Royal Charter has never been granted. It is most likely that confusion arose over the general use of the expressions "our Borough of Farnham and the town adjoining", and "Farnham and its Borough". The descriptions refer to the town and the congested houses enclosed by the town ditch.

The Charter of 1248 was confirmed in 1266, and again by Cardinal Henry Bauford on the 19th March, 1410. Although this Charter appears to have lapsed, it is significant in that it gave to the town the freedom to choose its own Bailiffs.

"They shall have all our ffaire of ffarnham at the feast of All Saints, whole without denial. They shall choose owne Bailiffs at their owne will and appointe and remove them as often as they please without contradiction of any of our ministers or officers whatsoever".

"They shall acquit of all our courts, savinge that they shall answer to the Lords of the Hundred at the Lawe Day, holden at our Castell of Ffarnham yearly to the Kings Chapitor without denial, and shall make their own courts, before their bayliffs, as they were wont to do before our bayliffs." "They shall have assise of bread and ale - unless the baker be condemned to the pillory or the brewer to the tumbrill - these penalties reserved to the Bishop."

This exemption from payments of assise recognised that the people of Farnham were townspeople, and could not be expected to plough and reap. Few had horses and carts. In recompense the following penalty was imposed: "In return pay a fee of £12 at Hocke day and att feast of St. Martin equal proportions."

This requirement to pay an annual fee of £12 was to become the source of a dispute between the Burgesses and Bishop Duppa, following the ravages of the civil war.

Without doubt the Bailiffs and Burgesses undertook their duties conscientiously and honourably, but their inclination to partake of lavish feasts out of income, led to a resolution in the reign of Elizabeth I restricting them from spending more than 2s 8d at a feast, but generally granting 20 shillings between the two Bailiffs and 4 shillings to the poor. The later payment was soon to be discontinued.

Some of the early feasts may have been held at the Old Goats Head public house, which was at the bottom of Castle Street. It was to become a popular coaching Inn during the 17th century, and a centre for music and entertainment.

It must be remembered that this was a period of immense religious upheaval. Roman catholicism was being replaced by protestantism. Bishop Robert Horne (1561-1579) was the first protestant Bishop of Winchester. His predecessor, Bishop John White (1556-1559) had been imprisoned for a while in the tower of London, and it was possibly from his desire to establish his authority, that Bishop Horne granted the Charter of 1566. The last to be granted, it was to last for two hundred and twenty three years.

The Charter was housed at the Castle for many years, but at some point "disappeared". Fortunately an early copy had been made and it was this copy that passed to Winchester in 1928, following the changes to the ecclesiastical boundaries and the establishment of the new See of Guildford. In 1997, the original Charter was said to have been discovered in the archives of a Roman Catholic Seminary at Emmitsburg, Baltimore, America. The method of acquisition, and the route taken remain a mystery.

At a subsequent formal exchange, the Charter was handed to the Episcopalian Bishop of Maryland, in whose Archives it now resides.

There have been other venison dinners, notably one held by the Borough of Kingston, Surrey. This was probably originated by Charles I in 1647, following the enclosure of the Royal Parks. The inhabitants of the town were excluded from hunting and given a buck, under Royal Warrant, in compensation. That dinner has now ceased and the Royal Warrant withdrawn.

Another dinner, also discontinued, was the annual Venison Feast at Andover, Hampshire. In 1859 about 30 gentlemen and tradesmen partook of the repast at the Mason's Arms, the buck being provided by the Earl of Portsmouth. The meal included fat venison, champagne, hot house grapes and a fine dessert - all for 3s 6d!

In spite of the obvious attractions of a donated buck, interest declined. At a feast on Tuesday, 5th September 1865, on this occasion at the White Hart Hotel, it was reported that attendance had reduced from the anticipated 80-90 to only 32. With this evidence before them, it was accepted that there was insufficient interest for the dinner to continue.

But the most prestigious annual banquet is one that predates that of Farnham. The Lord Mayor of London's annual Banquet can be traced back to the early 13th century. Usually attended by the Monarch, this

Part of the original charter of 1566 which established the first

corporation with the appointment of two Baliffs and twelve Burgeses sumptuous feast cannot be compared to a venison dinner, although in 1634 the extensive menu did include, among the pheasants, partridges, herons, fresh salmon and lobsters, a mundane venison pasty!

Bailiffs and Burgesses 1566 - 1789

The Charter of 1566 granted by Bishop Robert Horne created a new municipal body to run the temporal affairs of the town. It comprised two Bailiffs and twelve Burgesses, 'to be chosen from the best and most worthy of its inhabitants'. The first were chosen by the Bishop; thereafter they were to be chosen by the people. In reality they were chosen by the Bailiffs themselves. It was at this time that municipal accounts appear first to have been kept.

In the same year the Market House was built at the bottom of Castle Street. Incorporated into the upper floor was the lock-up, some 10 feet by 8 feet 6 inches, known as the 'Bishop of Winchester's cage'. Access for prisoners was by means of a step ladder. The alternative was to be hoisted by a rope. Understandably, the Bailiffs complained that they had difficulty in imprisoning drunken men. The comments of the drunks remain unrecorded. The Market House was erected by John Clarke, Senior Bailiffe, at his own expense. He was so angered by unfavourable comments from passing townsfolk who may have considered that a building supported by wooden pillars was unstable, that he added the inscription:

"You who don't like me, give money to mend me,
You who do like me, give money to end me."
A reasonable challenge from a benevolent man.

The duties of the Corporation are set out in a document under 'The Seale of the Towne'

"They have a three weeks court and try all cases under forty shillings.

They impannell and sweare a jury of All-comers and receave the whole profitts of the Marketts and Faires of the said Towne tyme out of mind. They hold their Court in the name of the Bayliffs and Burgesses, and use a Common Seale.

They levy a Rent within the said Towne upon certain Freeholds by the name of Borough-Rent unto theire own use.

They compell all people that sell Butter in theire Market to weigh eighteen ounces to the pound, and if they finde any that is unere eighteen ounces, they break it."

Tough action indeed, and it is not surprising that there was a tendency to be outspoken at their meetings. This is confirmed by the following extract from the Court Book of 1582:

"It is agreed by the assent of the greater number of the Bailiffs and Burgesses doo use any approbrious and unhonest speeches one to another, eyther in presence or out of presence, if it be proved by two lawful and honest witnesses, that then such person as is so abusing of any of his company shall be founde thereof guilty, and shall forfyte twenty shillings."

Note that they extract the maximum fine of 40s. How it would have been demanded and collected is open to conjecture, but the power to act in default appears, fortunately, never to have been tested.

That drunkeness was a problem is beyond dispute, and it may be coincidental that the presence of maltsters amongst the Burgesses may have influenced the local ruling that obliged the inhabitants of Farnham to buy their beer from Farnham brewers, under a penalty of 5s. Historically the Bailiffs and Burgesses had become accustomed to holding feasts at public expense. No doubt encouraged by the healthy state of their accounts, and unfettered by the fear of an annual audit with consequent public accountability, they met at the Market House on the 22nd September, 1605 and resolved that: "It is ordered and decreed that the bailiffs now chosen shall make a feast the next court day after the feast of All Seynts now next ensuing for the companie and Burgesses toward the charge of which the court shall contribute and paie the sume of ffortie shillings of current English money - and this order for ever in every bailiffs tyme afterwards shall remain and be used.

If once person or persons elected bayliffs shall refuse the usage and performance of the order and decrees above mentioned - that then he or they so refusing shall forfeyte and lose to the use of the towne fortie shillings of current English money to be levied of his or their goods by way of distraint."

The threat of a 40s fine may indicate that the decision was not favoured unanimously and that an inducement was needed in order to encourage support. Nevertheless it is this resolution that has been accepted as instituting annual feasts culminating in the establishment of the celebrated Venison Dinner. It was recorded in the Bailiffs Accounts as being a Town Feast, though it may not, in the early years always have been graced by the donation of a buck.

The Burgesses were just as concerned to indulge their spiritual needs. At that time it was usual for the most prominent families in the parish to have seats reserved in the parish church for their own use. The Burgesses were not to be outdone, and mindful of their perceived status, in a memorandum dated September 28th, 1607, they defined seats which were to be reserved for the sole use of Bailiffs and Burgesses. Anyone defying the order 'to forfeit 20s'. In lieu of payment they could take out a distress warrant.

King James I had visited Farnham on August 17th 1603, and resided at both the Castle and the Bush Hotel. He visited again in 1609, and when he came again in 1611, presented a buck to the town. Further visits followed, to such an extent that Bishop Bilson (1596-1616) was moved to enquire 'if the monarch looked upon Farnham as an Inn?'. The King's gesture of goodwill was continued annually, though occasionally in abeyance, usually by the resident Bishop.

The cost of the feast increased from the original 40s to £3 in 1612, and in the following year, when a buck was given by Lord Haddington, who was at that time a tenant of the Castle, the cost had risen to £4 2s, but a gallon of wine was included.

In 1617 there was no reciprocal gift of wine; the entry stating: 'Expense at the vendeson feast which my Lord Haddington gave to the town £3 2s

6d. Paid to keeper 3s'. But when, in 1634, it had risen to £10 19s 7d, it was resolved to restrict the amount spent at the feast to £14. The town was prospering and the resolution was ignored with the result that the cost rose to £23.12.8. with charges. The charges would have included the payment of a fee of 3s to the keeper for bringing the buck to the town.

The King's enthusiasm to visit the Castle is easy to understand. Farnham had the only episcopal palace standing on a hill overlooking the town. In addition, the extensive hunting was enhanced by the unrivalled panoramic views over the town and countryside.

The official gift of a buck gave added encouragement to the Bailiffs and Burgesses to indulge their desire to dine together on one great day each year. They were not unmindful either of their need of sustenance at their three weekly Court meetings. On these occasions the meals would have been modest to reflect the sobriety of the occasion, and conducive to the proper conduct of the town's affairs. The following is recorded in the Bailiff's Book of 1624:

"It is ordered the XXth of December in the yere written above by the Bailiffs and Burgesses of ffarneham that the Bayliffs shall be allowed (word unclear) every court day according to an order at the beginning of this book made the first day of October 1610 for and towards the making of a feast or dinner ev'ry Court day for such as the bayliffs shall invite according to the Order."

William Grene
(Other signatures) Robart Tomson, the m'ke of John Bookham
William Terrye, Robert Warner, George Wroth.

There was no requirement to hold public elections, and in the early years of the Corporation they continued in office until they died or decided to stand down, when a replacement was chosen.

The position was gradually formalised, as at their Court meeting each September they would decide those to be elected, or re- elected, either as Bailiff or Burgess, "all in accordance with the custom of the Borough and town of Farnham", and conclude their decisions by holding a celebratory feast on the first Monday in November. These feasts were somewhat modest, as the costs shown in their accounts ranged between £2 and £3 for maximum of fourteen gentlemen.

The Bush Hotel soon became the regular venue for the Venison Dinner until the late 1800's. In 1603 when James I became King of England there is a record of The Bush being an ancient Inn. There was thought to have been some sort of inn or ale-house on the site for over 300 years. The status of The Bush as an 'Inn' became the subject of a legal dispute when, in 1618, Sir Giles Mompessen, Patentee of Inns, took proceedings against one Harding, for keeping an Inn without a licence. Harding was not impressed, and defended himself by stating that The Bush was so old an establishment that it was 'an Inn by prescription,' and therefore did not need one of these newfangled licences.

At first the Kings Bench found against Harding, but a few years later, following a new application, the judgement was reversed. It was Sir Giles who had proposed the creation of a Licensing Commission, so it was not surprising that he had been appointed a Commissioner. But he charged such extortionate fees, and imposed such heavy fines, that scandal resulted. There was a demand for positive action. He was placed under 'house arrest,' deprived of his knighthood and fined £10,000.

In the early seventeenth century the principal trades in Farnham were connected with corn, wheat and cloth. But the growing of the local product 'kersie' for the production of cloth was declining as newer, and preferred, materials were being produced.

One well-known citizen and benefactor was John Byworth, a clothier, who was chosen as one of the town's Burgesses in 1606- 7 and in the years 1610-11, and 1615-1616 he was elected as one of the two Bailiffs. He had previously been elected Master of the Clothworkers Company for the year 1602-03. At his death in 1623 he left numerous bequests, including 13 cups, endowments for four almshouses, and 10s for a sermon to be given annually. One particular cup to the Bailiffs and Burgesses is described as "a silver cupp guilte valued at six pounds, thirteen shillings and four pence". This cup became known as the "Byworth Cup" and is held in high esteem, out of all proportion to its intrinsic value. This beautiful cup was gilded inside and had the inscription "The gift of Ma John Byworth unto the Bailiffs and Masters of the towne of Farnham and their Successors 1623."

The Byworth sermon became a casualty of history, but during the 1930's was revived by the Urban District Council to be given by the Rector at the Parish Church on 'Civic Sunday'.

John Byworth is buried at the Parish Church. His tombstone had the inscription "What I gave I have, what I kept I lost". The original tombstone has been lost, and there is doubt as to the accuracy of the wording, it being generally accepted that the mason made a mistake. A pun on the name 'Byworth' was adopted by the Farnham Urban District Council (created in 1895) when devising their armorial bearings, the motto becoming 'By Worth.'

The corn market had grown, and was soon to become the third largest in England, before being overtaken by the remorseless growth of the hop grounds. The hop plant had already been introduced into Farnham, sometime between 1573 and 1600 by a Mr Bicknell from Suffolk. When they were first grown in England is difficult to say, but it may have been in 1524. A clue may be found in the following traditional couplet:

'Turkeys, carp, hops, piccarel and beer,

Came to England all in one year.'

The tolls from corn and wheat were to become the principal source of income for the Corporation, reaching a peak of 90 per cent of their gross receipts.

On the accession of James I, Farnham had two parks; the Great or Old Park, on the West side of Folly Hill, and the New or Little Park which extended to the North and East of the Castle. Red deer were kept at the Great Park, while the Little Park was mostly for fallow deer. The Little

Park had been enclosed in 1376 by a fence made of split oakposts of sufficient height to prevent deer escaping. The ditch was probably inside the fence, with a 'deer leap' at the southern boundary of the park with St James' Terrace. The purpose of the deer leap was to allow feral deer, which roamed the district freely, to enter the park and become trapped, thereby supplementing the herd.

It appears that the game in the parks was not always adequately preserved, as in 1604 James I was displeased, and informed Sir George Moore, the Constable of the Park. But in 1606 measures had been taken to improve the keeping of the herd. The Monarch was appreciative and thanked the Bishop of Winchester for his care in carrying out the improvements. He would have travelled his kingdom extensively, and would expect to find adequate provisions for himself and his retinue at his destination. Farnham Castle with its deer parks would have satisfied his passion for hunting, while meeting his victualling requirements, so it is not surprising that in May 1608, Bishop Bilson leased to James 1 the Castle, the two parks and two chases. The monarch again occupied the Castle, but in 1619 leased the Castle and parks to Viscount Haddington for 21 years, "if the Bishop lived that long". The deer would have been hunted on horseback and shot with crossbows. Hounds were never used in the Farnham parks.

The Bailiffs and Burgesses continued to hold annual feasts. In 1633 the cost was £15 5s, the next year had increased to £23 12s 8d for 'ye great feast and charges'. This improvident increase resulted in yet another decision to restrict the cost of future dinners to £14. That these decisions were flexible was illustrated when in 1636, the kindness of the donor of the buck was recognised by the sending of a liberal present in return. In this instance the Corporation gave "six fat withers to our Lordship, £5 8s". On other occasions a sturgeon was sent to the Castle.

The feasts would have been all male, lasting for several hours, and undoubtedly convivial. Male clothing in the early 1600's would comprise a linen shirt and doublet, with a sleeveless jerkin worn over the doublet. Padded waistcoats were worn for added warmth, while knitted stockings were worn for both elegance and warmth. Footware ranged from soft leather pumps to sturdy boots. Hats of beaver, usually black, with high crowns and narrow brims would have been acceptable dress while at the feast, as they were only removed when in the presence of the King.

The indulgences of the Bailiffs and Burgesses were soon to be influenced by national events. Charles I had been enthroned in 1625 and was increasingly coming into conflict with the House of Commons. The differences were fundamental and seemingly irreconcilable. Following a period of mutual frustration, the monarch, in 1629 adjourned parliament and governed alone for eleven years. Then followed the 'short', and long', parliaments. Finally, in 1642 civil war commenced.

On the 22nd August Charles I had raised his standard in Nottingham, and the people of Farnham no doubt being aware of this, and most certainly aware that the Bishop was away "did, on Sunday, September 25th numbering about 100 men invade Farnham Park with dogs and muskets, hunting and killing large numbers of deer which were the property of the Bishop of Winchester". Palings were torn down and cattle scattered. The Keeper, John Tichbourne was threatened with death if he interfered. This action was probably more from a desire to obtain free venison than from a resolve to show support for parliament.

The result was that it gave an excuse for puritan troops to take over the Castle on October 22nd, but after a few weeks they vacated, and the Royalists seized their opportunity and took occupation. Initially Captain Weller declined to retake the Castle, but on December 1st, 1643 he summoned the garrison to surrender. They refused. Weller's men then blew up the main gate by petard, and fought their way in, forcing the Royalists to surrender. The design of the Castle suggests that it was intended as a fortified residence for the Bishops of Winchester. The circular keep is unusual, in that its walls sheath the usual mott, instead of standing on its summit, a device which would allow very little advantage to attackers managing to breach the walls.

During this period the Bishops were vulnerable and subject to acts of repression. The Bishop of Winchester, Bishop Curll, (1632-1647), a Roman Catholic, was stripped of episcopal office and became a fugitive. He made no attempt to return to Farnham Castle; instead he found sanctuary at the Palace of Bishops Waltham, from which he contrived to flee hidden in a manure cart, when the Royalists surrendered to the London Brigade. In 1650 he died.

For the next five years Farnham became the Headquarters for nearly 4,000 troops, comprising both foot soldiers and horse troops. Col. James was appointed military governor, with powers superseding those of the Corporation. Desertion among the parliamentary army was rife. General Sir William Weller, wishing to impose a deterrent, resolved to take action. The following is a report of a hanging on December 6th, 1642:

"Bartholomew Ellicott, sometime a butcher near Temple Bar, once a Captain in the parliamentary service and lately in the King's army, who was the week before taken prisoner, was hanged in the market place of Farnham for running away from the General's army, and carrying divers sums of money with him, which should have been paid to soldiers, and endeavouring to betray the town of Ailesbury. He died in miserable conditions, justifying himself in the acts, and condemning the council of war, which found him worthy of death, stoutly affirming that there is no popish army protected by the King". He was not the only soldier to suffer the death penalty as, Sir William had, shortly before, hanged a man from a tree in Farnham Park for mutiny.

During the war years the attitude of the people of Farnham was somewhat ambivalent, with no expressed stance for either side. According to Captain George Wither the Puritan leader, the townspeople were "creatures of the Bishop", and "malignants", i.e. Royalist in their sympathies. But conflicting evidence existed in that the Bailiffs, following a series of disputes with the curate, had paid a puritan preacher to give a lecture each Market day. This was a voluntary action on the part of the Bailiffs; the accounts showing "£3 6s 10d payd for Thursdays lectures from 5th day of April to 27th day of September 1627, as a free gift and allowance during pleasure." In 1632, £11 14s was given to the Thursday weekly lectures, at 4s 6d for the week.

Acrimony between the curates and the townspeople continued unabated; several curates being removed from office during these unsettled years. Sir William Weller in his 'Sufferings of the Clergy", states that a curate of Farnham had been taken into custody by order of the parliament, for opposing a new lecture that had been set up to be held on Market day. It appears that the lectures had ceased by 1652, as there is no record of further payments.

In 1644/45 the business of the town was virtually suspended, while under martial law and military government. The Bailiffs kept minimal records of market transactions, and civil court cases were rarely heard. The Market House fell into disrepair; lead was stripped from the roof to make bullets, while the streets were churned by heavy military carts and guns. Yet the traders prospered, no doubt from trade enhanced by the presence of soldiers, at times numbering as many as 4,000. The contracts for the provision of military uniforms would have been particularly welcomed by the local clothiers. The civil war concluded at the battle of Naseby on June 14th 1645, when Thomas Fairfax with his new model army defeated the government forces.

During the war years the Burgesses had been subdued, and in 1643 kept no accounts, as both Bailiffs had died, possibly in warfare. But they did not forgo their feasts, for in 1646 they expended £6 13s 6d, and in 1649 the cost rose to £11 17s 8d. The buck, if one was given, would have been at the discretion of the military governor.

The enthusiasm of the Burgesses to conduct the town's affairs had waned over the past three years. They had elected from their numbers two Bailiffs, but held no further meetings. Membership had shrunk to five. Where detailed accounts were kept, they continued to show expenditure on an annual feast.

One entry in 1648 records a payment to John Braybent for wine, tobacco and beer "when the General's soldiers were in town 1s 6d". This probably refers to the visit to Farnham by Oliver Cromwell on March 28th. It may have been a consequence of this visit that resulted in a resolution in the House of Commons on July 14th, "That it be referred to the Committee at Derby House, to take such effectual course with Farnham Castle as to put it in that condition of indefensibleness as it may be no ocassion for the endangering of the peace of the country". This decision authorised the official slighting of the Castle, and followed another small insurrection by royalists under the Earl of Holland. Peace was quickly restored, the troublesome Farnham Castle would be shorn of its defences. No sooner had the order been made to demolish, when soldiers garrisoned at the Castle sold as much woodwork, iron, lead and glass as they could dispose of. They were owed large arrears of pay and were not slow to seek recompense, with the result that one George Goodwyn who had purchased materials, and been slow to collect, found that the troops had beaten him to it!

The King continued his abortive attempts to reach a settlement with parliament. Two fiercely held and opposing principles met. The King would compromise but not yield. Further negotiations became pointless. Cromwell resolved the matter by riding to London, seizing the King and imprisoning him at Hampton Court Palace. The King escaped and fled to the Isle of Wight. He was recaptured and was taken to London in December 1648. On his journey he passed through Farnham and stayed overnight on the 19th December at Vernon House (formerly Culver Hall). It was said that "He came as a prisoner, suffering from ill treatment, shorn of every royal dignity, riding like a culprit with an armed guard each side of him". The Bailiff's Accounts for Michaelmas 1648 record that Robert Legge, an innkeeper, was paid five shillings and sixpence for "wood and candells when King laye at towne and when Col Users soldiers were there". The soldiers of the Kings escort were provided with "tobacco, pypes and bears" for a sum of six shillings and four pence. The King was so moved by the kindness of his blind host whom he held in high esteem, that he insisted on leaving a gift. He had few suitable possessions with him, but resolved the matter by giving his padded silk morning cap, which is today on display at the Museum of Farnham.

In January 1649 the King was executed.

That same year the Bailiff's expended £11 17s 8d on their feast. The Bailiff's Accounts were characterised by an introductory paragraph, in which the date was indicated by the phrase, 'in the Nth year of the reign of our sovereign Lord King Charles I'. Following the execution of the King, this was amended to, 'in the year of our Lord,' and was to remain unaltered for the next eleven years, after which the phrase was abandoned.

The Burgesses had always resented the limitations imposed upon them by the terms of their Charter, and would have seized any opportunity to expand their powers. They may have considered that the visit by Cromwell in 1648; the execution of the Monarch, and the relative neutrality of Farnham during the civil war created a favourable opportunity for a successful application. Whatever the reason, on December 17th, 1649 they resolved to petition for further privileges.

Their plea for: "Such other and further privileges and jurisdictions as shall be granted by letters patent or otherwise for the supreme power of the Commonwealth of England," was no more successful than it would have been under the Monarchy. The petition failed, and the matter was never raised again.

On April 20th, 1653, Cromwell, disgusted by the failure of the Rump Parliament to carry out promised reforms, dissolved it. But having destroyed the monarchy, he had nothing to put in its place. He was forced back upon military rule. Locally, the Bailiffs and Burgesses co-operated with the military governor. That they were concerned to improve the condition of the streets is evidenced by a decision in 1654, agreed by the townsmen and Bailiffs, "that every man against his own household pave ten feet towards the kernel (a central gutter) for the whole breadth of his house, and that the Bailiffs of the town are to pave the rest to joyne to the ten feet either side - stones can be taken from the Castle wall for this purpose". This vandalising of the Castle was at the discretion of Captain Brewer, who was entrusted with its demolition. The same year the Town Feast was to cost £30. 1s.

In the aftermath of the war, trade had been returning to normal. Farnham with its network of roads and easy access to London had spare milling capacity, and the government decision to prohibit milling within forty miles of London, gave the needed impetus to develop local facilities to supply the lucrative markets of London and Chichester. Both towns had been puritan strongholds, and the knowledge that the townspeople of Farnham had invited a puritan preacher to give lectures on market days before the war, made business relationships easier to establish. Further evidence of the acceptance of presbyterianism in Farnham arises from the governments ordinance on the 5th March, 1648, to establish a parochial presbyterian form of church government, with elders appointed from each parish to assist the minister. The legislation had passed the House of Lords on the 14th March, but was not acclaimed generally as it was imposed from above and was not the result of natural progression. The Farnham elders included Mr Piggott, Mr Searle and Nathaniel Wroth, all names of Farnham Bailiffs at the time. One family, Bicknell, produced one minister who practised his ministry from his home.

During the 1640's the Burgesses had voted themselves two feasts a year. In addition to the indulgent Town Feast, they had a more modest feast to celebrate their re-election. Religious strife continued unabated. John Clapham, Vicar of Farnham since 1623, was disruptive to the occupying soldiers, and came under fierce attack. One Joshua Clapham, presumably a relative, spoke up for him, but relented and issued the following retraction on January 20th, 1650:

An Apology

"To all whom this may concern. Whereas I, Joshua Clapham of Wrecclesham, was this day overtaken by my tongue and being overruled by passion suffered my tongue to speak amisse against the bayliffs and burgesses of Farnham, theis is to certifie that I confess it to be an error in me and acknowledge myself sorrie for same."

If Joshua Clapham had been overruled by passion, the Bailiffs and Burgesses were most certainly not. Scant consideration was given to the financial burden falling upon the poll and rent payer, as the cost of the Town feast rose to £46 16s. 6d. in 1652, with a further increase to an all-time high of £51. 5s. 1d. in 1653. Possibly, there were pangs of conscience, but whatever the reason, the Burgesses were enjoined, once again, to resolve to contain their excessive expenditure on their Town Feasts. In 1654 they resolved not to exceed £20, and for the next twenty years this resolve was not broken.

Farnham was now, by degrees, becoming the great corn market for the central part of southern England. The cloth trade had been in serious decline for several years, while hop yields were increasing. and were to provide the enormous wealth that was to accrue in the next century.

The Bailiff's Accounts were in a healthy state. The position in 1664 when both Bailiffs had died, and it appears that expenditure had exceeded income by £20. 9s. 5d., had not been repeated. The Bailiffs salaries had increased from 20s to £10 per annum, with the addition of three Under Bailiffs. It was to be one hundred years before the next "out of pocket" balance was to be recorded, though in somewhat different circumstances.

With Cromwell's death in 1659 came the end of the Commonwealth, and the restoration of the monarchy in 1660. The Bishops were re-appointed. Bishop Brian Duppa (1660-1662) who had retired to Richmond during the years of the Commonwealth, was appointed to the See of Winchester, and took residence at Farnham Castle. He found the Castle in a ruinous state.

During the years of the Commonwealth the "Lord of the Manor" titles and possessions had been auctioned off to the highest bidders. "Farnham" presented a lucrative acquisition and had not escaped. This was only the second occasion that the Farnham Manor had passed out of the hands of the Bishops. The first was in 1551. Bishop John Ponet (1551-1553) had been appointed to replace Steven Gardiner. He immediately gave up his episcopal Manor in return for an annual income of 2,000 marks. In June 1551, several Manorial irregularities were reported, including that of Farnham. Edward VI swiftly deprived Ponet of his See, re-possessed the Manor and re-appointed Steven Gardiner.

In 1658 the Manor of Farnham had been sold to John Farwell and James Gold for the sum of £8,145. 8s. The Bishop quickly regained ownership. There is no record of any compensation being paid. This was, presumably, regarded as a case of 'rough justice' as Gold complained to parliament, requesting restitution, without success.

In an attempt to raise money to pay for the restoration of the Castle, Bishop Duppa repudiated the rights of the Bailiffs to collect rents and tolls, and claimed them for himself. In addition he sought to increase the £12 annual fee paid by the town since the Charter of 1410.

In 1661 he had granted a lease of all the fairs and markets with the tolls and profits thereof to one Thomas Kilvert, a Londoner, for a period of 21 years. Kilvert appointed bailiffs to collect his rents, but was forcibly restrained by the townspeople. A series of actions for assault and battery followed, in which the townspeople allowed judgement to go by default. The Bailiffs and Burgesses refused to abandon their rights and privileges enjoyed since the middle ages, and declined to co-operate. The dispute festered until Bishop Duppa's death in 1662.

In the same year Bishop Robert Morley (1662-1684) succeeded to the See. He had an eye to public relations, and presented a buck to the town, for which the Bailiffs responded by sending a sturgeon and wine at a cost of £5. 12s. This benevolence did not resolve the impasse, as the Bishop, although kindly disposed to the town had, while accepting the surrender of the lease, granted another one. The townspeople had been in some difficulty in pursuing their case, as their charter had 'been mislaid in the late troublesome time,' and they could only allege that they were a Corporation by prescription, and had always collected and enjoyed the tolls themselves. Throughout the turmoil, the venison feast - the sign of an underlying desire for harmonious fellowship - survived. In 1664 another buck was given, and the Burgesses spent £1 7s 6d at Mr Maberleys for fish, and gave 15s to Mr Newbold and Mr Halls for bringing the buck from the Lord Bishop.

Kilvert, no doubt feeling his position was now secure, tried to collect a toll of peas. As a consequence there was a disturbance, and at the Surrey Quarter Sessions the following October Kilvert was found guilty of 'making a riotous assembly', and fined 5 shillings.

The townspeople had now managed to find their charters, and the security of Kilvert's lease became doubtful. Meanwhile, Kilvert was negotiating for a transfer of the lease to Matthew Roydon, a man who, at a later court action, was to describe the people of Farnham as 'cunning jugglers.' Kilvert naturally made light of the difficulties he was having. Writing to Roydon on the 23rd October, 1665, he stated: "As for the grant they talk to have, it is so lame and blind a cheate (having neither signe, scale, nor witness to it) as they are ashamed to show anybody. Kilvert once again attempted to take a toll by sending his agent, John Mosier on November 10th, 1665. On this ocasion he was set upon by the Bailiffs and Burgesses, and roughly handled. Townspeople joined in. At the ensuing Quarter Sessions on January 9th 1666, they were fined 12d each. All were drapers and maltsters, and appropriately armed would have presented formidable opponents.

It is significant that two of the participants - Robert Bicknell, jnr, and Abraham Lee, had been named jurors for the Farnham hundred that year. Conversely, Christopher Newland of the 'Rose and Crown', who was a county Bailiff, had sided with Kilvert. Here we see further evidence of the political resistance to ecclesiastical control of secular affairs, that was to continue throughout the life of the Corporation. Although discontented, the Burgesses carried out their duties steadfastly, and in 1664 expended £50 13s 9d on "repairinge the Market House". In addition to their annual feasts, they made occasional payments for fish. Their accounts for 1666 show a payment of £2 5s 'for sturgeon eat at all times'

It was not the Bishop and his leaseholders who were proceeding directly against the Corporation. In the Hilary Term 1665, a Quo Warranto was brought by the attorney-general against the 'borrougholders' of Farnham, for usurping the rights of the crown in taking the tolls in the market. The reason is given by both leaseholders, Kilvert and Roydon. Kilvert, writing in 1665 that a Quo Warranto will force the inhabitants to exhibit their title, if they have any, and Roydon in 1667, saying that he had been advised that it would be more difficult for the inhabitants to defend a Quo Warranto than an action by the Bishop. If the town had been waisted, the Bishop could have produced charters of the crown granting him the market, and the leaseholder would have been secured. The inhabitants continued to plead that they were a borough by prescription, and that they were preparing their evidence. They were hesitant about appealing to a record they had of Bishop Horne's Charter of 1566. It appears that they had only a copy of it, not the original. But the Bishop was maintaining that he had been granted the market: had the status of a 'Prince Bishop', and the Corporation could not remove these privileges. In reply the Bailiffs and Burgesses said that they did not seek to remove these privileges, but to prove that certain rights had been transferred to them. They did not claim to have a gallows, but said they were a body politic with a common seal, had a right to hold a court of frankpledge twice a year, and could deal with all actions in the borough except felony, and to have their own courts every three weeks. They claimed also the right to choose 2 Bailiffs each year "for good and wholesome governing of the town". Last and most important, to hold a market every Thursday and two fairs every year, and to take the tolls thereof. In fact, for many years three fairs were held: Holy Thursday for horses, cattle, sheep and hogs, and on June 4th and November 13th which were restricted to horses and cattle only.

The case was finally tried before Chief Baron Hale, the rest of the Barons of the Exchequer, and a special jury in 1669. The jury found for the defendants, the town, and signed a non ulterius presequi. The Corporation emerged victorious. There remained a financial settlement to be agreed. Up to 1666 the Bishop had received payment from his lessee. Since then the Bailiffs had paid nothing. In 1671 they paid £66, being 5½ years rental at £12 per year. To obviate further conflict, the matter went to arbitration, which was concluded in 1672. Under the terms, Roydon surrendered his virtually worthless lease to the Bishop, and received compensation of £210 from the town, in consideration of waiving all future claims. There is a record of the Bailiffs raising the money by way of a loan at 3%.

The Burgesses sent a conciliatory salmon to his Lordship. To the Bishop's credit, his determination to restore the Castle did not diminish. He was responsible for overseeing extensive works of renovation at a cost of £30,000 and deserved the accolade "the restorer of paths to dwell in". The internal works of remodelling resulted in a reduction in the dimensions of the Great Hall from 66 feet by 44 feet to 49 feet by 30 feet. He led a life of strict asceticism, to the extent that the room he chose for his bedchamber was a small room some 8 feet square, in the basement of Fox's tower.

By this time the Bishops were no longer central to the policy making of the state. Although they were Lords Spiritual in the House of Lords, they had become administrators of the church, but still retaining immense authority.

It should have been obvious to the Burgesses that they would have to adhere to the terms of their Charter, or put the future of the Corporation at risk. Notwithstanding this, interest in managing local affairs appears to have slackened. There had been difficulty in maintaining the level of Burgesses to the maximum of twelve, possibly due to their apparent indifference to their obligation, while the financial standing of the Corporation was, to say the least, obscure.

The accounts, which ran to two or three pages each year, were prepared by the Bailiffs and signed by the Burgesses as being 'settled and allowed by us'. Standards of literacy were low, and there are examples of Burgesses agreeing accounts by 'making their mark'. There are numerous alterations and arithmetical errors. No funds were created and no balances brought forward. Under the terms of the 1566 Charter they were to receive "the whole profitts of the Marketts and Fairs of the Towne tyme out of mind". These monies, together with the tolls of assize and rents, comprised their income to manage the affairs of the town as they saw fit. Any deficit they would make good, while any surplus would be theirs to share out. For the present all was well, there were ample funds to maintain the annual 'share out', but the writing was on the wall. If the Bailiffs were aware of the impending dramatic changes in the trading patterns shortly to affect the town, they had no inclination to take any action to safeguard their financial future. They continued with their meetings at the Bailiffs House, exercised their right to hear cases of debt: to inspect and seal leather sold in the market, to taste bread and beer, and inspect weights and measures; in the case of a trader selling butter underweight, to break his scales. They exercised their power to levy fines of up to 40 shillings, but as the charters were not 'Royal' they were denied the power to impose higher penalties. They also received rents and tolls from the property and markets in Castle Street and The Borough.

Castle Street was the location of the Fish Cross and the Butchers' Shambles. It was the presence of the latter that may have led to the imposition of a fine of 12 pence upon any person throwing the bodies of dead animals into Bear Lane.

If there was an air of complacency it was understandable. It can be seen that conflicts of interest may have arisen, in that a desire to hold an annual feast, and to meet obligatory expenses had to be balanced against a possible need to ensure a respectable end of year balance for division between themselves.

The annual income from corn and wheat tolls appeared to be sustainable for an infinite number of years. In 1657 they were able to extend their hospitality by expending £4 9s on a dinner for the Justices at the Bush Hotel, while managing to retain a balance of £20 8s 5d to be divided. In 1675 the corn toll was £165, with the aggregate receipts for the year amounting to only £201 6s, but in 1694 the highest point of prosperity was reached, with receipts from tolls totalling £370 out of a total income of £400 - a percentage of 91.8.

This volume of trade should be taken in perspective, as it was a far cry from the 12th century when as many as 400 loads of wheat drew into town. Huge loads left for London drawn by as many as sixteen horses. There were now some 300 acres of hopgrounds in Farnham. In 1682 they were producing incomes of £40-50 per acre, and for the best quality as much as £100. Farnham soon became famous for producing the best hops on the rich upper greensand soil. In spite of the vagaries of the weather, no other crop was so capable of making the grower so wealthy in so short a time. The result was to be the construction of elegant Georgian houses in West Street and other parts of the town centre. Bishop George Morley died in 1684, having disparked the Old Park and leased it to farmers, (subsequently reduced to a single tenant in 1798, when Bishop Brownlow North leased it to John Henry Gill for 21 years, at an annual rental of £70). He had also provided a water supply to the Castle from a hill above the park. The system was extended to provide a 'pure sweet water' to the town via a lead 'conduit' running down Castle Street, and terminating in a chamber fitted with a pump, at the junction with The Borough. The access flagstone can still be seen in the colonnade outside the building which is now the Nationwide Building Society. Bishop Morley's successor, was Bishop Peter Mews (1684-1706) 'the fighting Bishop', so-called because he had taken an active part in the civil war, and had been wounded at the battle of Sedgemoor in 1685. During the period between the death of Bishop Mews in 1706, and the occupancy of the Castle in 1707 by his successor Bishop Johnathan Trelawny, (1707-1727) the tenants had made free with timber and deer. No doubt they were attempting to assert 'rights' considered to have been established during the period of the Commonwealth when there had been no form of management control. The new incumbent determined to regain control of his lands, and appointed one Heron as Steward.

Heron set out to restore the Bishop's rights. His actions were unacceptable to the countryside who rose against him. The tenants drew up another 'customary', claiming to be socagers (Anglo-Saxon term for the free tenure of land by the peasantry) with rights, including cutting timber on their own copyhold lands. Hop growing was burgeoning, and they wanted to use the land to grow hop poles. Heron denied these 'rights'. Kirby, the Woodward of Bishops Waltham, drew up a number of 'articles against Heron', alleging him to be immoral and a Sabbath breaker, and stating that he had threatened to throw one of the Bishop's Officers in a blanket, if he ventured to come to the Castle. Heron tried to defend himself, but was unable to resolve the dispute, and was eventually replaced by Edward Forbes, whom it was thought would have a better attitude when dealing with timber problems.

By this time, the lawlessness that was rife in the forested parts of Hampshire and Berkshire had spread to Farnham, and was to strain relations between the Bishop and the townspeople for a number of years. The only visible effect upon the Burgesses, was their inability to maintain their number, which frequently fell to as low as eight, and in later years much lower, together with a disregard of the need to balance the annual accounts. One figure of expenditure which did, remarkably, remain constant was the recorded cost of the Town Feast, which remained at £12 from 1680 to 1738! One year of note is 1697 when the accounts show an income of £307 10s 10d which included £273 5s from tolls of corn and other dues, the remainder being small rentals and fees; the surplus of £179 IIs 5d presumably being disposed of by the annual 'distribution.' It can be seen that without the disproportionate income from corn and wheat tolls, the financial future of the Corporation was insecure.

The Bishops looked upon the Castle as a summer residence, and spent most of the winter journeying in foreign parts. Understandably, in their absences the tenants made most of their opportunities to pillage. In 1710 the first Private Enclosure Act was passed, thereby allowing Bishop Trelawny (1707-1721), to obtain permission to enclose the lands of the Old Park. It was at this time that a band of masked men with blackened faces, calling themselves the "Waltham Blacks", made constant attacks on The Holt and Waltham Forest, stealing deer and cutting down trees. There seemed to be no way of combating them, for in 1717 they turned their attention to Farnham Park. In that year, Edward Larby, one of the Bishop's officials wrote: "The park is seriously disturbed, and now Holt is destroyed, will suffer every day more and more by a pack of beggarly thieves, not sportsmen, who kill for their skins more than the now reasonable meal". He told the Bishop that he had intercepted a covered wagon carrying away venison, hens, poultry and plunder of all sorts. In 1718 with the Park coming under repeated armed attack, Bishop Trelawny placed an advert in the London Gazette offering a free pardon and reward to any informer whose evidence led to a conviction. But he had to retract as he could not commit the King to such a potentially damaging course of action.

In October 1721, sixteen deer poachers broke into the Park, and carried off three deer and left two more dead on the ground, shooting and wounding a keeper. Several suspects were arrested, two of whom were sentenced to the standard penalties of a day in the pillory, a years imprisonment, and a fine of £20. The comrades of the imprisoned men bound themselves to each other by oaths, chose to be under a mock kingly government, and elected a very stout, enterprising and substantial gentleman whom they took for their Leader - their 'King'. Once again and in greater numbers, they broke into the Park and took eleven deer, leaving as many dead behind, and made into the town with their haul at 7.00am on the market day in open triumph. They made no attempt at concealment, except that they were masked and wore gloves. Their leader was known as 'King John'. He was proud of the achievements of his band and made known to the townspeople his objectives and apologised to them for any disturbance. The identity of 'King John' was never established.

During the numerous raids, lodges were destroyed, timber burned, even cows shot at. In the end troops had to be stationed in Farnham. Their presence proved so effective that the 'Blacks' left Farnham alone, and turned their attention back to Waltham.

In 1722 the notorious Black Act was passed. This act imposed the death penalty on those convicted of stealing deer, robbing warrens and fishponds, cutting down trees and pulling down hop bines. After seven men had been hanged, the poachers, it is said, only became more outrageous. The Act was soon repealed, as it became recognised that the penalties were draconian and unacceptable.

A watercolour of the Market House in 1761.

In 1730, one Black Will, living in The Bourne, whose dog had been taken away by Henry Bone, the park keeper, went into the park with some companions 'armed with gune, a mathook and other weapons with full intent to break open the Lodge'. The outcome is uncertain, but he was presumably repulsed. Meanwhile at Waltham Forest, the Keeper was being routed, and the park ravaged. In 1750 when all the deer had gone, Bishop Benjamin Hoadley (1734-1761) declined to restock, 'as the deer had caused enough mischief already'.

While the Bishops were having acute problems with the poachers, the Burgesses were facing increasing difficulties with achieving a healthy balance with their accounts. Tolls from corn had plummeted as the hop grounds expanded. Also, corn was increasingly being sold by sample, and it had become cheaper to use water transport to convey corn in bulk to London. They had no claim upon the hop duty as this was collected by Customs and Excise.

As the hop industry expanded, there was a need to secure an abundant supply of hop poles and ropes. Firs were planted at Crooksbury, but there was little enthusiasm, and the trade was not developed to its potential. The planting of firs was soon discontinued. Long Garden Walk became the official 'Rope Walk,' and by an Order of 1754, the making of rope was confined to this area. The walk stretched through the length of Long Garden Walk to the opposite side of Castle Street. The rope was produced by a team of three men, two walking backward with the rope between them. They twisted the strands and closed them, while the third man used a marlin spike to pack the strands tight.

William Gilpin visited Farnham in 1775. In 'Western Tour' he describes the view from the terrace of Farnham Castle: "Town may be called a vale of hops, for we saw nothing but ranges of the plant ....the hops and the vine in a natural state, are among the most picturesque plants. Nothing shows so much the prejudices of names as the value fixed by Farnham hops. The Farnham farmers agree every year on a secret mark which they affix to their own bags. The value of the hops spread under our eye from the terrace was supposed to be at least £10,000."

Later, writing in 1778, Daniel De Foe describes the serious decline in the corn trade: "Farnham, except for Hampstead and London, the greatest corn market in England, particularly for wheat, of which so vast a quantity is brought hither, that a gentleman told me he once counted 1100 teams of horse, all drawing waggons or carts loaded with wheat; every team of which is supposed to bring a load, which is 40 bushels, in the whole, 44,000 bushels. But there has been a considerable falling off, on account of the sea carriage to London."

Although the Corporation was still in existence, its members had virtually ceased to exercise any powers in conducting the affairs of the town. The Vestry had gradually taken over items of expenditure, and was now the acknowledged authority.

From 1739 to 1755 the Burgesses had confined their feasting to a post-election feast at costs ranging from £1 10s 6d to £2 7s 5d, a modest expenditure in keeping with their reduced circumstances. From 1756 even these post-election feasts were forgone. Surpluses were under £15, and in 1771, 1772 and 1775 they had deficits of 2s 3d, £3 14s 6d and £2 1s 8d respectively. There was no prospect of a return to the halcyon days at the beginning of the century when surpluses of over £100 were the norm, while figures of over £200 were not uncommon. From the 1760's with their numbers reduced to as low as two, and with no financial reserves, their days were severely limited.

From 1771 sole responsibility fell upon Andrew Bristow and William Shotter. Expenditure had been contained to the minimum, but there was no possibility of any improvements. Their final accounts for the year 1778 show a small surplus.

The accounts of Mr Andrew Bristow for year ending Michaelmas 1778.

	£	s	d
Receipts			
Borough Rente (51 properties)	1	16	5½
Outstandings	0	18	0
Shamble Rente (5 lettings)	5	14	0
Bridge Rents (Tilford Bridge)	0	13	4
Sheep Coops	5	0	0
Sign Money (Public Houses)	0	0	0
Shew Money	1	6	0
Toll wheate,			
(Two loads and one sack)	21	6	6
Barley	0	0	0

Oats	0	0	0
Pease			
(six bushels and one half)	1	6	0
	38	0	3½

	£	s	d
Disbursements			
To half a year's land tax for the Markete due at Ladyday 1778	2	0	0
To half a year's Lease Rente due at Ladyday 1778	1	4	0
To half a year's land tax for the Weighing Engine due at Lady day 1778	0	9	0
To Samuel Jackson a Bill	5	2	6
To a Team two days fetching Gravel) and three labourers two days each	1	8	0
To Poor Rate due at Michaelmas 1778	1	7	6
To half a years Land tax for the Market due at Michaelmas 1778	1	0	0
To half a year's Lease Rente due at Michaelmas 1778	1	4	0
To half a years Land tax for the Weighing Engine due Michaelmas 1778	0	9	0
To Henry Strcate a Bill	0	3	1
To Philip Avenell a Bill	1	10	0
To one years Fee Farm Rente due at Michaelmas 1778	9	12	0
To Stewards and Council's Fee	1	1	0
To Servants Wages (Harry Collins and Richard Hack)	8	0	0
	34	10	1

	£	s	d
Receipts	38	0	3½
Disbursements	34	10	1
Dividende	3	10	2½

19th December 1778 Accounts settled and allowed by us
Signed: Andrew Bristow. William Shotter.

The need to carry out repairs to the two stone bridges at Tilford had become a matter of extreme urgency. During the reign of Queen Elizabeth, the bridges had been described as being in a ruinous condition. In an endeavour to provide a permanent solution, Bishop Horne had executed a Deed whereby the rental from a piece of land at Tilford, called Bridgeland, was transferred to the inhabitants, on condition that the bridges were maintained in a sound state of repair. The annual rent of 13s 4d called 'bridge rent' had been handed over, but in latter years the bridges had not been maintained sufficiently, and there was no available money to complete the repairs. The Corporation, not having functioned for the previous ten years, was in default: William Shotter was indicted for failing in his duty. Consequently, on July 27th, 1789 the following deed was executed by him, (he was a partner in the firm Shotter and Evans, Solicitors) and delivered into the hands of Bishop Brownlow North (1781-1820):

"I resign and surrender unto the hands of the Honourable and Right Reverend the Lord Bishop of Winchester my office as surviving bailiff of the borough and town of Farnham together also with the tolls, customs, dues, profits, privileges, advantages and emoluments to the said office, belonging or appertaining, and all rights and title thereto ; and I humbly entreat his lordship that he will be pleased to accept this my resignation and surrender."
"William Shotter"

Thus came to an inglorious end the tenure of the Corporation, but it did not signal the end of the Venison Dinner.

The collection of tolls reverted to the Bishop. Few records exist, but in September 1806 two Commissioners of the Land Tax Redemption Office contracted with Bishop Brownlow North by redemption by him of £4 8s land tax, charged upon certain estates - tolls of the Market and lease of rents. It is recorded in 1812, that the Bishop's agent collected tolls and rents amounting to £20 16s. In the same year under the terms of an Indenture dated 7th May in the fifty second year of the reign our Sovereign and Lord King George III, a lease of 21 years was granted by the Bishop to John Manwaring, John Holiest and Geo Coldham Knight of Lower House, of the building called the Cage, situated within the Market House together with a piece of the ground (10 feet 6 inches by 9 feet by 8 feet 6 inches) situate on the South West front of the said building, with full liberty to use as a commonplace for offenders against all laws and statutes of the realm. By this time the original stepped ladder had been replaced by a well constructed staircase with winders. An annual rental of £6 was payable to the Lord Bishop, at the feast of St Michael and the annunciation of the Virgin Mary in equal proportions, free of all parliamentary and other rates, taxes and impositions whatsoever, and agree to maintain and repair the building.

The lessees were required to provide a key to the building, to officers of the Court Leat or Court Baron, with free access to allow them to imprison offenders. At the expiry of the lease they were required to peacefully and quickly, surrender and yeald up to the Bishop or his successors.

In 1837 the Market Tolls demanded by the Lord of the Manor, payable to his agent, Messrs Hook & Frost were:

For every sack of corn, I pint of same.

Stalls, according to size. From 6d to 2s 6d.

Coops for pigs, 6d on market days: 1/- on fair days.

Ditto for sheep, 1/- to 2/6d.

The Vestry 1789-1866

The Vestry had existed throughout the years of the Corporation. Meetings were held in the church vestry; hence the name. Its purpose was to manage the affairs of the church, both spiritual and structural, but during the 17th and 18th centuries these duties had been gradually enlarged, to the extent that there was more concern with the preservation of order, and the maintenance of the town's social fabric, than with the salvation of souls and the conduct of church services. The secular duties gathered since the 16th century, included the care of the poor, control of vermin, maintenance of highways, the keeping of workhouses, the enlarging or building of an infirmary, and paying for arming and training of local militia men. Their range of responsibilities and duties, greatly exceeded those of the Bailiffs and Burgesses. The Churchwardens received legitimate expenses, but did not organise the Venison Feast, which was organised by an independent committee, which may have included, from time to time, some who held office within the Vestry. The Vestry had, in addition, the power to purchase places for employing the poor, and the authority to appoint Surveyors of Highways. Most importantly, and unlike the Burgesses, they had the power to fix and collect a number of annual rates.

The Venison Feast was no longer a 'freebie' of the local Corporation. It was now a private venture, with tickets purchased by those who wished to attend. The Vestry kept detailed accounts of its activities, with surpluses husbanded for future years. This is not to imply that there was never any discontent in ecumenical circles. In 1771 a dispute arose over the collection of the poor rate in respect of Farnham Castle. In a letter to Bishop John Thomas (1761-1781), dated February 2nd, 1768, it was stated that the Poor Rates had been very high of late with many complaints. As a result the rate books had been investigated. Several lands and tenements which should have been rated to the poor were not. During this investigation it was found that his Lordship had been rated at £60 per annum for the broad and meadows, but there was no charge for the Castle or Park. It had been reported that paupers had been received by the parish from the Bishops. In particular, one, since his Lordship had come to the See, had been maintained by the parish until she died. It appeared that both Bishop Jonathan Trelawny (1707-1721), and Bishop Charles Trimnell (1721-1723), had paid parochial rates for the Castle and Park for the years to 1724, but since that time until Lady Day 1768, no charge for parochial taxes have been made. At Lady Day 1768 when the Poor Rates were being made for the previous half year, it was recollected that upon the present Lord Bishop coming to the See, Mary Lunn, an old servant of the Castle, who had lived there as a yearly servant for more than thirty years, had been sent from thence to the workhouse; maintained for two years, and afterwards buried at the expense of the parish. "Whereupon a lawful inspection of the preceding church book was made, and the void and neglect discovered". The Overseers requested the Bishop to pay the Poor Rate for the Castle and Park due for the half year from Michaelmas 1767, to Lady Day 1768. The Bishop refused to pay. Similar requests for payment for past years were also refused. At that point the Overseers of the parish were doubtful whether the publication of all the rates due could be proved, "especially as the late parish clerk just dead". Undeterred, they journeyed to Chancery Mews to seek legal advice on how to proceed, from Mr Powell, their legal attorney. They were successful in obtaining a Distress on the Goods and Chattels of the Bishop for the last half year only. i.e. From Lady Day 1770, to Michaelmas 1770. On completion of the legal process Robert Trimmer and Thomas Eyre, two of the Overseers of the parish obtained a Warrent of Distress on the Goods and Chattels of the Lord Bishop, and on the twenty second day of December 1770 went to the Castle to levy the Distress, which amounted to the sum of ten pounds. The debt was discharged when the Bishop instructed his agent, Mr William Hay, to pay. The yearly servant, Mary Lunn, would have been accommodated in the workhouse in Middle Church Lane; built in 1726, it soon became inadequate to meet demand and was replaced in 1790 by St. Andrews House, Hale Road, at a cost of £4,000.

The existence of widespread acute poverty among the labouring classes in Farnham was recognised, with the result that almshouses were provided by some of the benevolent brewers and tradespeople. The first, and perhaps the most notable, were The Windsor Almshouses in Castle Street. Founded in 1619 they provided accommodation for "eight, honest, old impotent persons". A puzzling restriction. Clarification can be obtained by referring to legislation. The classification 'impotent person' is to be found in the Poor Law Act 1601. It defines as 'impotent', those who are willing to work, but found to be inadequate, and, presumably, as a result, unemployable.

The desperate plight of the poor, was to trouble the consciences of charitable individuals and bodies throughout the life of the Vestry. Numerous local charities were created, while nationally the nuclei of the Friendly and Building Society movements were being established. The headquarters of the Cumberland Friendly Society, and the Farnham Freehold Land & Buildings Society were housed in the Goats Head public house, which became a staging post of the Gosport Diligence Stagecoach.

The enormous changes in trade brought about by the decline of the corn trade, and the cloth industry, and the steady upsurge of hop growing were soon to be reflected in the proceedings at the Venison Dinner, and in the occupations of those attending.

The 300 acres of hop yards quoted by Aubrey in 1673, had increased to between 800 and 900 acres in 1780, according to Oulton in his 'Inventery', so much land being needed, that building was not allowed on land suitable for growing hops.

When occupying the Castle, Bishop Brownlow North attended the dinners, and it was during his speech in 1784 that he is alleged to have made an offer to donate a buck each year, in the hope that poaching of deer in the Park would cease. This is a delightful story, but the Bishops were worldly, with a deep understanding of human nature, and it is doubtful whether the annual gift of a buck to the obviously wealthy, at a sumptuous feast, would have had a restraining influence upon those needy persons who were never to be invited. Nevertheless, it was this "conditional offer" that ensured the continuation of the donation, the tradition of the dinner, and led to that year being acclaimed the origin. Throughout the nineteenth century this dinner was regarded as being "Number 1", with the incumbent Bishop being the Guest of Honour. To this day, the numbering starts from that date. The reason why the early feasts were disregarded has never been explained.

"K", writing in the Surrey Magazine in 1900, about the Bush Hotel, states: 'upstairs overlooking the picturesque borough is the famous banqueting Hall, in which is held each year the famous Venison Dinner. The festival originated in the generosity of Brownlow North appointed to See of Winchester in 1781. 116 years ago the worthy folk partook of the first of those dinners, and each succeeding year the reigning prelate of Winchester has upheld the quaint custom of presenting a fat buck from the leafy glades of Farnham Park. Over fleeting years the banquet has lost none of its old-time flavour or importance'.

Bishop Brownlow North retained a genuine concern over the plight of the poor, for in his Will he left £300 to the poor of Farnham.

To a government looking for additional sources of income, the expansion of hop growing and brewing presented an easily taxable commodity, and too good to miss. A duty on beer had been introduced in 1660, the year of the restoration of Charles II. There followed various taxes on malt, and in 1710 a duty of 3d per lb was imposed on imported (Flemish) hops. This was extended in 1734 to include hops grown in England at 1d per lb. Thereafter the duty varied from year to year. By 1801 it had been increased to 2½d per llb. Stringent controls were devised to overcome avoidance of payment. A penalty of £40 could be imposed for using 'twice or oftener the same bag, with the officer's mark upon it'. Other offences included the removal of hops before they had been bagged and weighed; concealment of hops, and privately conveying away hops with intent to defraud.

While the duty received from hops provided a significant income for the government, it was subject to wide fluctuations caused by the vagaries of the weather, and the ravages of disease and pests. This is well illustrated by the following table showing the duty paid on hops from 1740 to 1750, in the Hampshire and Farnham district:

1741	£1,611	1746	£870
1742	£2,916	1747	£3,009
1743	£1,860	1748	£2,536
1744	£2,002	1749	£2,795
1745	£1,678	1750	£951

Before the development of Weyhill Fair, Hampshire, the Farnham hops were taken to Stourbridge Fair, Stourbridge Common, to the north east of Cambridge town. Originally known as Steer Bridge, it became Sturbridge or Stirbitch in the 18th century, before being changed to Stourbridge by writers in the 19th century. Prodigious quantities of hops were sold at the fair, which enabled them to set prices for the whole of the country. Hops were also transported there from Chelmsford, Canterbury, Maidstone and London.

With the establishment of the fair at Weyhill, described as the 'Greatest Fair in England', dramatic changes occurred in both marketing and the control over prices.

Farnham hops were highly rated, generally obtaining higher prices than those from other counties, including Kent. It was said that the Farnham planters, 'were careful not to let the hop stand so long as to take on a decidedly yellow colour, or to give out a strong degree of brightness'. Gangs of pickers were employed during the first three weeks of September; the hops being placed in pockets weighing 168 Ib. Trading at Weyhill began on the 12th October and continued for several days, but generally restricted to four.

The Farnham growers formed a small consortium to reduce transport costs, and, as a safeguard against robbery on the journey, leaving via Crondall Lane, had their gold and banknotes sewn into their waistbands by their wives who accompanied them. In 1737 the Farnham growers purchased Blissimere Hall, Weyhill, for their sole use to avoid paying demands for rental increases for the booths. For many years it had been a proven 'right of common' on Blissimere Hall Acre. Unaware of the legal position, the Farnham growers had paid an annual rental to the Churchwardens of Weyhill. On discovering their error, when the next demand for rental was made for 'injury to pasturage', they refused to pay. Legal action was threatened, but not pursued.

One Farnham grower, James Stevens, following a narrow escape from a highwayman, engaged an armed guard to escort him on his journeys to and from Weyhill. This protection was so successful that other growers asked him to carry their money as well. Stevens, an astute business man, soon realised that taking responsibility for other peoples' money had commercial possibilities. In 1806 he opened Farnham's first bank in Castle Street. But there were fluctuations in the market, and during one downturn when there was a run on local financial institutions, he allayed customers' fears by placing a number of sovereigns on top of an open bag of hops. Customers seeing the bag 'full of sovereigns' were re-assured, and continued their custom. Eventually, the stresses of running a bank proved tiresome, and in 1815 Stevens sold out to James Knight, a prosperous brewer, who increased the capital investment and expanded the business. In 1868 James Knight & Sons decided the business had reached the stage when more prestigious offices were warranted. The resulting building, an "Elizabethan House" designed by Norman Shaw, R.A. comprising four storeys at a cost of £18,000, was thought to be too pretentious, and became known as 'Knight's Folly'. In 1886 the business was sold to Capital and Counties Bank for £9,000. In 1918 Lloyds Bank absorbed all 473 branches of Capital and Counties, and opened another branch in Farnham. The two branches merged in 1919 on the former

Knights premises, which were demolished in 1931 when the present building was constructed, and remains so to-day, fittingly, in Castle Street.

William Cobbett visited Weyhill frequently. On 15th October, 1826 he wrote: (Rural Rides) "The crop of hops has been, in parts where they are green, unusually large and of super-excellent quality. The average price of Farnham hops has been as nearly as I can ascertain, seven pounds, and that of Hampshire and Surrey hops (other than those of Farnham) about five pounds also. The prices are, considering the great weight of the crop, very good; but, if it had not been for the effects of 'late panic' there prices would have been a full third, if not nearly one half higher; for although the crop has been so large and good, there was hardly any stock on hand; the country was almost entirely without hops".

Many Farnham families made their own beer. Cobbett estimated that a small labouring family needed 274 gallons a year. This would require 15 lbs of hops.

Not unexpectedly there were occasions of widespread drunkeness. One such day in Farnham was 'Hop Sunday', when there was a convivial atmosphere with beer flowing freely. The newly appointed Bishop Sumner (1827 - 1869) objected strongly, and succeeded in stopping the event. It was last held in 1828. As a result the Bishop received much abuse from the imbibers.

This hostility did not deter the Bishop from his benevolent activities. It had for some time been the custom of the Bishop of Winchester to distribute bedding and clothing at Christmas. Bishop Sumner gave orders that at Christmas 1828, this should be done as usual. When the day came, the Castle was literally besieged by applicants, the court-yard so crowded that it was difficult for those who had received their blankets to pass out, and make way for others. This continued during the day. There was a great deal of grumbling, and no gratitude, for all looked upon 'the gift', as it was called, as a right. The Bishop and Mrs Sumner were both present themselves during the greater part of the distribution, and determined that such a scene should never be enacted again. Before another Christmas came along, a clothing club had been established. Demand was enormous, some 500-600 clamouring for their parcels. Such was the degree of poverty in the town.

William Cobbett was critical of the Bishops, but had praise for Bishop Sumner, as described in his letter to the Hampshire parsons published in the Political Register dated 15th January, 1831. He writes: "I have, at last, found a Bishop of the Law Church to praise. The facts are these. The Bishop, in coming from Winchester to his place at Farnham, was met about a mile before he got to the latter place, by a band of beggars, whom some call robbers. They stopped his carriage, and asked for some money, which he gave them. But he did not prosecute them; he had not a man of them called to account for his conduct, but the next day, set twentyfour labourers to constant work, opened his Castle to the distressed of all ages, and supplied them with food and other necessaries who stood in need of them. This was becoming a christian teacher."

With the agricultural community prospering, and still, apparently, with an assured future, the needs of a developing urban centre received attention. The Farnham Gas Company had been formed in 1834 with an initial capital of £3,000, and the right to supply gas to properties within the parish of Farnham. They were now looking for contracts. A meeting of their Directors, and the Inspectors for Lighting and Watching, took place on the 4th August, 1834 to consider an offer to set up and keep in repair and light 40 lamps with gas, or 60 lamps with oil, in the several streets of the town, from dusk on 30th August, 1834 to 5th September, 1834 for £25. Agreement was reached with the Gas Company to fit and supply 40 lamps with gas.

Meetings of the Inspectors for Lighting and Watching record incidents far removed from the social conditions of to-day. At a meeting held on the 7th September, 1835, Watchman William Stanford reported that between 11.00 and 12.00 o'clock the previous night as he was going his round he saw Richard Young, George Young and Charles Hook near the Market House. George Young had a ferret in his hand, which he (the Watchman) endeavoured to catch sight of, (suspecting it might have been stolen), when he was thrown down by Richard Young and George Young, and on getting up again Richard Young attempted to strike the Watchman, but the Watchman attempted to defend himself with his staff, and knocked Richard Young down. The Inspectors feeling that any assault on, or resistance to, the Watchman should be visited by punishment, ordered a complaint to be made to the Magistrates, with a view to affecting a conviction. At a hearing on the 5th October, 1835, both men apologised and offered to pay all expenses and not to molest again.

The responsible and benevolent attitude of the Lord Bishops toward the people of Farnham, found expression in many practical actions. Following the example of Bishop Morley in providing a water supply, albeit primitive, to the town, Bishop Charles Sumner, in 1836, granted 20 acres of land at Lawday House Common to William Birch (builder), Andrew Collyer the younger (Gentleman), H.G.Gray (grocer), J.Knight (banker), and William Vaughan (surgeon), for the purpose of providing a spring supply of soft water to the inhabitants of Farnham town, by means of the formation of a joint company. The initial share capital comprised 100 shares at £20 each. There was no doubt about their resolve to get water to the town, as the purpose of the company was to provide in the conducting of water from the springs into proper reservoirs, by means of cuts, drains, tunnels, conduits, feeders and other aquaducts, from thense by pipes to the homes and premises of the inhabitants of the town of Farnham. Meetings of shareholders were held variously at the Lion and Lamb Inn and the Board Room of the Town Hall. The company undoubtedly prospered, but expansion was restricted, and in 1898 they were taken over by the Wey Valley Water Company.

During the first half of the nineteenth century the production of hops reached a plateau. A brief report in the 'Standard' of 11th October, 1848, depicts vividly the enormous growth in production. "Exported at least 4,500 pockets from Farnham alone. Brightest new Farnhams £5-£5.10s per cwt; for 1847 - £4-£4.10s cwt, discoloured ditto £2-£3 cwt. Duty computed £210,000, to be collected nationally."

At that time there were twenty five hop fairs in England and Wales, and it follows that betting upon the aggregate amount of duty payable was a popular event. The supremacy of hop growing and brewing locally over other agricultural pursuits was reflected in the choice of names for public houses, e.g. 'The Hop Blossom,' ' The Hop Bag' and 'The Pocket of Hops.'

The secular affairs of the town continued to be managed by the Vestry, which was now reaching its zenith. As new Acts of parliament were passed, the inhabitants looked to it to take action. Public meetings were held in the vestry of the Parish Church, and advertised by affixing a notice to the principal outer door of the church, and by publication during divine service on a Sunday. On the 2nd August, 1830 a petition had been submitted to, "The Churchwardens of and for the Market Town of Farnham" to hold a public meeting to determine whether "provisions contained in Act made in the 11th year of the Reign of late Majesty King George IV entitled 'An Act to make provision for the lighting and watching of Parishes in England and Wales' shall be adopted."
Sgd.

Jas Stevens	C.J.Horne
George Trimmer	Jas. Shotter
Thos. Eyre	N.Newnham
Geo. Miller	Saml Andrews
R.Shurlock	Robert Clark
R.Drinkwater	W.Crump

All were noteworthy local traders and professional men. The result was that at a Meeting held in the Vestry, on the 18th August at 12.00 noon, with the Rev C.J. Horne in the chair, it was resolved (1) by a majority vote, that the provisions of the Act be adopted. (2) The highest amount of rate in the pound that the Inspectors shall have power to call in any one year, shall not exceed one shilling and four pence.

The following were elected as Inspectors: Robert Clark, William Crump, John Knight, George Miller, Henry Nichols, William Pinke Paine, James Stevens, George Trimmer, Joseph R. Williams.

Thomas Eyre was appointed Treasurer, and William Mason, Secretary. At the first meeting held at the Savings Bank office on Wednesday evening on the 18th August, William Beagley and Thomas Cole were appointed as Watchmen and Night Patrol, at a weekly wage of 12 shillings each, and James Steer to assist during any emergency.

The town area was to be patrolled every day from 25th March to 29th September from 11.00 at night, till four in the morning, and from 29th September to 25th March, from 11.00 to 5.00 in the morning. Their duties included calling the hour, every hour. At a later meeting, the Watchmen were to be reprimanded for not calling the hour. In their defence they pleaded 'hoarseness'. The Vestry exercised firm control over their Committees. At a special meeting held at the Treasurer's House, Lion and Lamb Inn, on the 19th February, 1850, by the Superintendent, one John Reed was charged for 'misbehaving in his duty as Watchman in night of Monday last'. Reed was deemed to be more of a disturber of the peace, than a preserver of the peace, and was dismissed from the office of Watchman and Policeman.

Following another request to the Vestry in 1836, a 'Board for Repair of Highways of the Parish of Farnham', had been formed. Ordinary meetings were to be held at the Bush Inn. James Stevens was appointed Chairman, with John and James Knight as joint treasurers. In 1877 a rate of sixpence in the pound was fixed. Other public meetings were held to elect Overseers of the Poor, Churchwardens, Members of the Burial Board; to nominate constables (subject to the approval of the magistrates) and to fix rates for Lighting and Watching, Relief of the Poor, Highways and the Church Rate. All accounts were subject to annual audit, and public examination.

The Rate for the Poor Law differentiated between 'buildings' and 'land'. In 1832 the government, aware of the serious levels of unemployment in rural areas, endeavoured to relieve the problem by passing 'An Act for the Better Employment of Labourers in Agricultural Parishes until the 25th Day of March, 1834'. 0ne provision related to hop lands: That for every six acres of hop ground the occupier shall find employment for one man before he shall be permitted to work out his position of the Poor Relief Act. At the time, the Rate was 1/- in the pound. In Farnham many of the unemployed would have been made redundant as the cloth industry declined, with insufficient alternative employment available.

For many years labourers were paid ten shillings for a six day week. A comparison can be made with 20th century labour relations by referring to a decision taken at a special meeting on the 13th December, 1838, for the purpose of 'considering the propriety of raising the wages of labourers on highways as a consequence of the high price of bread'. An increase from 10/- to 11/- was agreed, with discretion being given to the Assistant Surveyor, to give 12/- where there were large families.

The annual Venison Feast continued to be organised by a committee of some of the prominent traders and businessmen in the town, with their own elected Chairman and Vice-Chairman.

As one public indicator of the quantity of hops harvested was the amount of duty paid, it only needed an occasion when growers, brewers and businessmen, got together in a congenial atmosphere, for gambling to take place. It will readily be appreciated that it was now appropriate for the date of the 'new' dinner to be advanced from November to a date before picking commenced. During the 18th and 19th centuries there was no legislation specifying a Close Season for the slaughter of deer, but there was an 'unwritten law', respected by sportsmen, that confined the hunting or stalking of stags to the period 12th August to 12th October, and the hunting of hinds from 10th November to the end of March.

Compliance with both restrictions would be met by arranging the dinner during the latter part of August.

The third week was the popular choice, as this enabled the betting to be conducted with knowledge of the likely yeald and quality of the growing bines, while being unaware of the prices to be achieved. Most dinners were held on a Tuesday.

During July and August of each year, detailed reports appeared in local and agricultural newspapers, evaluating the effects of the weather upon the growing binds, with estimates of likely yealds. In 1851 "The Sussex Express, Surrey Standard, Weald of Kent Mail, Hants and County Advertiser" contained the following report: "Farnham 24 July: The hop reports are very conflicting, some grounds are reporting better, while others are decidedly worse, and certainly the prospects of a crop are in a most critical state." Farnham's economy continued to rest upon the wealth arising out of the production of a single crop. For the workers, a succession of bad summers would result in mass unemployment, with little prospect of an alternative.

With no Corporation involvement, the Feast had became an established Hop Betting Dinner, with the virtual guarantee of the gift of a buck from the Bishop for good measure. Bets were laid at the August dinner and paid out at a dinner the following May, the Chairman for the year being the individual whose bet was closest to the aggregate duty. A book listing the bets was kept at the Bush Hotel until the 1960's. The following is an extract from the entry for 1850.

"The following gentlemen agree to subscribe to a sweepstake of 5/- each, the nearest to receive the stake. Mr Parson, Mr Parminster, Mr F. Thumwood, agree to go halves in the sweep. Names and money listed. Memorandum: All bets made at the Venison Dinner payable at the May Hop Betting Dinner, that is on the hop duty. The nomination of each gentleman is opposite each name, the one nearest to be chairman, and all his expenses paid for the day.

All bets entered in this book to be paid at the May dinner.

Mr Betts	200,500	0	0
Mr G. Goodman	212,500	0	0
Mr H. Andrews	189,500	0	0
Mr W. Brown	189,760	0	0
Mr Jas Knight	165.690	0	0
Mr C. Andrews	195,591	0	0
Mr E Parminster	197,104	13	9¾
Mr E Parsons	184,759	19	11¾
Mr T. Thumwood	203,711	0	0
Mr J Andrews	215,000	0	0
Mr H. Lampart	225,000	0	0
Mr G. Trimmer	199,911	0	0
Mr E.Y. Knowles	215,100	0	0
Mr Reynolds	214,777	0	0

A number of side bets are recorded.

Examples:

Mr Knight backs his nomination against Mr T. Trimmer (as for Venison Dinner) for £1.

Mr Brown backs his nomination against Mr Andrews for £1.

Not all bets were for cash:

Mr J. Goodman bets Mr Trimmer a new hat for 21s the duty of £200,000.

Mr J. Andrews bets Mr G. Trimmer a new hat (best beaver) 24s the duty pays £200,000 to be had of J. Goodman (a local retailer)

Mr Thumwood bets Mr C. Betts bottle of wine that Mr C.Andrews is chairman of the May meeting. All bets were against the duty payable nationally. In 1850 the estimated duty payable on Farnham hops only, was between £9,000 and £10,000.

13th May 1851 Hop Betting Dinner

The following gentlemen agree to dine at the Bush Hotel the second Thursday in May 1852, for the purpose of settling all debts made on the hop duty under a forfeiture of 4s each for non-attendance.

G. Andrews	"	"	£155,000
G. Trimmer	"	"	£149,900
H. Andrews	"	"	£171,000
W. Parsons	"	"	£161.000
J. Goodman	"	"	£185,000
B. Stevens	"	"	£110,000
T. Thumwood	"	"	£173,611
C. Andrews	"	"	£157,600
J. Knight	"	"	£135,000
C. Falkner	"	"	£111,111
C. Betts	"	"	£170,000

The nomination of each gentleman is opposite each name, the one naming the nearest to be chairman, and all his expenses paid for the day. All bets made and entered in this book to be paid at the May dinner, date as above".

Dress at formal occasions was changing considerably. Hats were not worn. Jackets were becoming fashionable - smoking, Norfolk - and were slowly evolving into the dinner jacket and black tie of the 19th century.

Much has been said about the hop growers, the hop fair and hop betting. What of the hop pickers? At the end of August, hundreds of workers crowded into Farnham hoping for employment. One local grower employed as many as 2,000. Their living conditions varied enormously, as many of the itinerants had no available lodgings.

In 1857, a Mrs Young of Aldershot, visiting Farnham for the day, wrote of her experience: "Hoppers slept under the old Market House. This place is raised on piles, and under it littered down with straw like cattle, were the 'hoppers'. Now, it must be understood that these were not 'home pitchers' but strangers, a chancer ragged band, who allured by hope of gain, had travelled from every county in England to the harvest. The growers do not recognise this class nor provide for them in any way, even the straw they had was given in benevolence by Mr Andrews the farmer-butcher at the place, and by no means a matter of right." "When I strolled amongst them but a few had risen; men, women and babies were huddled together in the straw , while here and there a poor family squeezed themselves into an empty china crate, and one or two, finding long empty baskets, had set them on like sentry-boxes, and were sleeping, so protected a little from the cold. One family newly awakened, and consisting of a granny, a young husband and wife, with their little child, were seated under a large cotton umbrella; dirty, but gaudy shawls were rolled around their feet, and as I saw their bronzed faces the scene came back to me of the French steamer Caire, on her way from Stamboul, with groups of slaves for the governor of Mitylene. By half passed five, all Farnham was alive with hop pickers."

It cannot be said that the hop growers suffered similar privation, but the burden of the Hop Duty did not fall equally upon all engaged in the industry. Spirited representations to parliament resulted in the setting up of a Committee to Report on Hop Duty. In August 1857 they produced their Report. They found that the production of hops required a greater expenditure of capital and the need to employ more labour to the acre than any other branch of agriculture. The majority of witnesses (these included growers, maltsters and brewers), estimated the cost of cultivation, up to the time of picking at from £22 to £30 per acre. The expenses of picking, drying, etc, were generally estimated at from £1.16s to £2.4s per cwt, including the Excise Duty of 19s 7d 72-100ths, which might be regarded as a cost of production. A moderate computation would be upwards of £2,000,000, spent annually, on the production of hops nationally. Annual aggregates of income varied wildly. In 1855 the duty was eight times that of 1854, showing that the crop was most precarious, with widely fluctuating yealds.

Several kinds of hops were produced in England, but they could be divided into two classes, namely; those of inferior description, for example, grown for most part in the weald of Kent, and Sussex, and upon other inferior soils, and those of superior description principally raised in Middle and East Kent. Market price of the inferior hop was 25-50 per cent lower than the superior.

The fact that the Excise Duty was imposed uniformly upon both classes, formed constant ground for complaints from growers of crops on soils of inferior quality, as they generally produced a greater quantity per acre, thereby attracting the greater amount of duty. The tax was charged in October, and was payable in two instalments - 15th May, and 15th November following. As the duty was a charge on quantity, it was greater when the crops were heavy and, as a consequence, prices low. The wealthier growers therefore had an advantage over their poorer competitors, who were often obliged to sell cheaply, just prior to the duty becoming payable. Numerous applications had been made since 1800 for the duty to be postponed. In fourteen years the applications had been allowed, and payment deferred or remitted. The Report of the Committee was that the duty should be abolished. Importers fared rather better. The import duty amounted to £2.5s per cwt, with the positive advantage over the home grower, that the imported hops were placed in bond with the duty payable, if, and when, they were sold. At this time, imports and exports were almost balancing each other. Farnham was coming under pressure from the Kent hop grounds, who had lower production costs, partly due to their adequate supply of wood suitable for poles and making charcoal. But all growers had identical problems in their constant battle to control pests. An old Kentish verse includes the lines:

First the flea and then the fly,
Then the mould, then they die.

The basic character of the town centre as a market had not changed significantly. Neither had the strategic importance of the road system which linked London with the coastal ports. Army battalions passed through the centre frequently. In May, 1862 when the 2nd Battery of Artillery passed through the town on a Thursday, en route for Aldershot, they found the streets occupied by a cattle fair, and caused some little crowding among the gaping rustics, in charge of the sheep and pigs. Change became inevitable, when a transfer of property was agreed under the enabling powers contained in the Ecclesiastical Leasing Act 1858. Bishop Sumner had, in 1865, conveyed to the Farnham Market House & Town Hall Company Ltd., the site of the Market House, the hereditament and the Market Fair and other tolls. All for the sum of £426.10.0.

A subsequent, but predictable, decision by the Town Hall & Market House Company Company did lead to an irreversible change in the fabric of Castle Street late in 1865, when the Market House was demolished. A replacement was to be constructed fronting The Borough, on part of the site of the Goats Head public house. This building had been devastated by fire in 1796, and conveyed to the Town Hall and Market House company in 1864.

The site of the old Market House continued to be used for market purposes, as the right had not been extinguished.

Following many years as an outlet for the market garden produce, it today retains Farnham's link with its historic past by providing a unique site for market stalls in the town centre.

The new Town Hall and Corn Exchange comprised, on the ground floor, a large hall which could seat 500 and was 70 feet by 36 feet with a ceiling 30 feet high, and four shops. The first floor formed the Town Hall. The structure was widely condemned as having no architectural merit, and in the 1930's was replaced with the present building, which does not contain a hall. The design was by Harold Falkner, the renowned Farnham architect.

Accounts of the Venison Dinner were now appearing in the local press. One of the first was in 1863, when on Tuesday, 25th August, at the Bush Hotel, forty three gentlemen sat down to consume the fat buck, "a splendid fellow," given by the bishop of Winchester and well served by Mr Ballard. Mr James Knight presided, and Mr Aylott, a visitor, ably filled the Vice-Chair. The usual loyal, patriotic and complimentary toasts were given and responded to. Several capital songs were sung, and 29 gentlemen put down their names in evidence of their intention, if possible, of doing honour to the Bishop's buck at the Bush next year. The next year Mr Knight again presided, with Dr Wilton, Vice-Chairman. Forty five guests enjoyed the first of many sumptuous feasts provided by the new host, Mr E. Bromley. Edward Bromley, whose father had been a stagecoach driver on the route from London to Portsmouth, ensured that the food and wine partaken at the Venison Dinner for the next twenty five years were of the highest standard. He became acclaimed for his cuisine, described as 'recherché', a term used in the 19th century for foods which were extremely choice or rare. The dinners were held in the Assembly Room, a large room overlooking The Borough, with seating for 140 guests, the walls being decorated with the antlers of previous repasts.

One element of the 'tradition' had changed significantly during the past year. The recommendation of the 'Hop Committee' to repeal the Hop Duty Act, had received the support of parliament.

Following a reduction of the duty to 1½d in 1860, the Act was finally repealed in 1862. Betting ceased, otherwise the ritual remained unchanged. The Bishop continued to provide the venison, and, when in residence, to preside, while most of those attending would today form the nucleus of the local "Chamber of Commerce". The local press, by now well established, reporting on events during 1865, noted that Her Majesty Queen Victoria had visited Farnham, and stayed at Moor Park house, the delightful home of J.F. Bateman. She had visited Waverley School, but not the Castle, where she had stayed during her visit in 1856. Mostly, her short journeys to Farnham followed official visits to Aldershot military camp. The following year it was reported that on Tuesday, 21st August, 1866 this interesting and time-honoured event took place in the Assembly Room of the Bush Hotel, when tradesmen of the town assembled to partake of the 'venison feast' which was honoured by one of the most sumptuous dinners that had ever graced the occasion. The local importance and advantage of these social gatherings, at which every branch of the commercial interests of the town were represented, could not be too highly estimated, for they believed it was at one of these meetings that the erection of the present Town Hall, and the construction of a new railway line were first mooted. One of the most important of these advantages was the interchange of friendly feeling and good-will between different classes of the community.

In order to encourage this social friendship, the residents of Farnham Castle - they being generally the episcopal lords of the manor - had usually contributed a buck from the herds of the park to the inhabitants of the town, which was served up at the annual dinner. The present Bishop had, with his usual liberality, contributed a buck. Shortly before six o'clock when dinner was announced, the company gathered in the Assembly Room, and delighted in the tasteful decorations of the tables, it being evident that no effort had been spared by Mr Bromley, the worthy host, to afford the utmost satisfaction. The wine, dinner, and dessert were of the choicest description, and not at all inferior to that supplied at the opening of the new Town Hall".

The Bill of Fare was impressive, and by to-days standard, excessive:

First Course: Mock turtle and Julien Soups, Turbot, Salmon, Filleted Soles and Whiting.

Second Course: Haunches of Venison, Venison Pasties, Roast Beef, Boiled Beef, Boiled Leg of Lamb, Roast Lamb, Boiled Chickens, Roast Chickens, Ham, Tongue, Ducks, etc.

Third Course: Cutlets, Oyster Patties, Lobster Patties, Curried Rabbit, Cotelottes de Homard, Rissoles, Croquettes, etc.

Fourth Course: Grouse, Leverets, Ducks, Hares, Cabinet Pudding, College Pudding, Cherry, Greengage, Apple, and Plum Pies and Tarts, Cheese and Celery, etc.

Fifth Course : Grapes, Pines, Melons, Plums, Filberts, Cakes, etc.,etc.

The Chair was taken by James Knight, Jnr, Esq., and the Vice-Chair by R.T. B Barrett Esq. Also present Messrs. G.V.Knight, - Knight, Holtzapffell, Crook, D.Edwards, F.C.Birch, Rupert Varndell, R.Beale, Caldman, Woodbourne, Hodgson, Gilbert, E.McCutchan, J.McCutchan, F.Andrews, Lowndes, A.E.Lucy, Bowler, Lindsay, John Nash, J.Nichols,Jnr, Hackman, Raggett, Michaux, J.Bentall, Aylwin, T.Hoare, Vine, Johnson, T.Smith, Potter, Eyre, Bryant, etc., etc. Mr Gilbert, Sen, the well-known toastmaster fulfilled his duties in a most admirable manner, assisted by his son, Mr Harry Gilbert, who superintended the serving of the dinner. Mr Frank Percival, a London professional singer entertained with some first class singing. Grace was said by the Chairman, and after the removal of the cloth, dessert was placed on the table in abundance, which, together with the various viands, reflected the highest credit upon Mr Bromley. The Chairman gave the usual loyal toast, which was enthusiastically received. In proposing 'The Prince and Princess of Wales', he expressed a hope, that some at least of those present might live to see the Prince of Wales on the throne of England, with the Princess of Wales as his Queen. Many of them had had the opportunity of seeing them, not only at a distance, but at Aldershot, near their own town, and also had opportunities of reading in the newspapers of the kind, courteous, and, nevertheless, royal manner, in which they had met their mother's subjects, and proved to the public that when he (the Prince) becomes King of England, "he will walk in the steps of his mother," and hoped that he would make as good a king as she had been queen. (Cheers) The Vice-Chairman proposed the health of 'The Lord Bishop of Winchester and the Clergy of all Diocese'. He spoke first of his Lordship, for 'it was true that the way to an Englishman's heart was down his throat'. While thanking his lordship for his liberality he emphasised that his respect did not rest upon the trifling foundation of the annual gift of a buck. His Lordship had spent a long working life among them as a neighbour, and the nation had known him as a christian man, anxious for the welfare of others, and as a prelate he had done much, and was still doing much, to prevent the widening of a breach between man and man.

Farnham was very fortunate in having, amongst their inhabitants, gentlemen who acted with the Bishop in carrying out anything that tended to promote their good. The toast was received and drank with enthusiasm, three hearty cheers, and "one cheer more". The song that followed, by Mr Frank Percival - "I'd rather be a Soldier", cannot have been intended as a personal reflection! The Chairman then gave "The Army, Navy and Volunteers". "He thought they all knew something about the army." "At all events they had defended our shores in the past, had been sent further afield to preserve the peace, and to keep our shores in a state of quiet. Our navy was progressing, and it was only last week that the channel fleet had been cruising, and proving itself to be in a state of efficiency when called for service. Our volunteers were now in a same state. They had recently had a meeting at Farnham, and he was pleased to find out that they had appointed a captain, and that their numbers were fast increasing. They were still armed with the muzzle-loading rifle, but he had heard that some of them were contemplating bringing the breech-loading rifle into use, even before our army. He was pleased that at least some of our army were going to be armed with the weapon, as in the last war with Germany it proved itself to be most efficient. If Englishmen were armed with the weapon, he thought then they might then sit at home and smoke their pipes in peace. (Hear, hear)." The toast was drunk with hearty cheers." Others were allowed to speak: Mr Arthur E.Lucy: "I am sorry there are no representatives of the army or navy here, but I am proud to say that I am one of the volunteers of England. I was one of the first volunteers in Farnham, and hope and trust that the day will soon come when the British Government will see the necessity of devoting a little more time to our volunteers, and require a great deal more of them, so that we may see them more equal to the militia and army (Cheers)". (The 'Militia' were recruited under the Lord Lieutenant of each county. The duty was removed from them and transferred to the War Office in 1871, when it was dropped from the toast. The Volunteers regarded the Militia with disdain.) Mr Holtzappfell, who held a commission in one of the London volunteer corps, also briefly acknowledged the toast, and concluded by singing "The Volunteers of the Island". The Chairman followed by proposing the toast of the evening, "Prosperity to the Town and Trade of Farnham". Since they last met at the annual venison dinner, he was pleased to say that great progress had been made in the town. They had got their Town Hall, which would bring many together both in private and in public; and he thought they ought to thank the directors of the undertaking for their exertions. He alluded to the drainage of the town, and expressed the opinion that it was necessary; hoping, too, that it would be done thoroughly. Many steps yet remained to be taken, the most important of which was the election of the first Local Board. He had looked down the long list of persons nominated, and found amongst them many good men, who would not spend the public money recklessly, but who would do some good for the town, though some had said "Let us not have it". They should be specially careful in voting, so that they have the "right men in the right place" (Hear,hear). The town was progressing , and he was sure the trade would do likewise.

The toast was drunk upstanding, and with three times three.(Three cheers in earlier times, now changed to three sharp claps repeated three times)

There followed a song by Mr Frank Percival, "Kathleen Mavourneen".

Mr Crook in rising to respond said that he associated himself with the Chairman's congratulations on the improved business of the town. It had been proved to them by a statement in the newspapers respecting the great increase in the postal business of the town, than which there could be no better proof of the magnitude of the business transacted. He then referred to the Local Board of Health, of rather the Local Board of Government, and observed that there was a great misapprehension that the Local Board was formed purely for effecting improvements, whereas it was for the government of the town, to remove nuisances and obstruction, and to render the town a credit to all (Hear,hear). He was sure the most conservative person present could not but acknowledge that there was room for improvement, and that there was no occasion to go to an enormous and unnecessary expense unless it was required.

It required no chemist to assure them that pure air and pure water were of the most vital importance to good health. He could say that a glass of pure well water could scarcely be obtained in Farnham; and if a friend, who a teetotaller, called on him for a glass of water he would at all times rather "mix" for him (laughter). He did not believe there were few springs in the town but were contaminated with animal matter, and he spoke not from mere idea, but from actual experience. He thought that it was essential that they should have a proper system of drainage. He would say that they should have all nuisances removed from their sight, so that they might present a pleasing aspect to visitors who arrived in the town. He agreed with the Chairman that there were many things calculated to offend the sensitive organs of the ladies; there was no mincing the matter about it, for, as the poet observed, "Out of the fulness of the heart the mouth speaketh". He concluded a practical and thoughtful speech with continued applause. A song, this time by Mr Moody - "The Tight Little Island". A song was also called from Mr Bromley, the host, who sang "The Ship Nancy". Mr H.Potter proposed "The Health of the Chairman, Mrs Knight and family", and in doing so "endulged in some highly flattering and congratulatory terms." This was followed by a comic song by Mr Ginger: "I've Lost my Missus". The toast was cordially received, and duly acknowledged by the Chairman, who assured the company that he was always ready to do what he could for the town and his fellow townsmen, and thanked them for drinking his health and that of his family. Yet another song. This time by Mr Lindsay: "The Land of our Ancestors". The Chairman then proposed "The Health of the Vice-Chairman", and paid a high compliment to that gentleman, both for the interest he took in the welfare of the town, and for his qualifications and usefulness. The toast was drunk upstanding, all joining in the chorus of "He's a jolly Good Fellow". The Vice-Chairman replied suitably. The toasts continued with "The Ladies", with a response by Mr Johnson. (The dinner was still an all-male affair, ladies not being admitted until the next century). The toast of "The Hop District", responded to by Mr Nash. "The Country Gentlemen", responded to by Mr R. Beale. "The Press", responded to by Mr A.K.Lucy. "The Health of Mr and Mrs Bromley", responded to by Mr Bromley; while "The Next Merry Meeting", received general acclamation. There followed a mixture of toasts, songs and recitations by several of the gentlemen present, including Mr Frank Percival, whose rendering of "My Pretty Jane", and "The Anchors Weighed", were much admired and enthusiastically encored.

The interesting, and no doubt exhausting, event was brought to a close about twelve o'clock, when the company separated, hopefully with carriages awaiting.

The poll for the new Local Authority was imminent; it was the result of a public meeting held at the Bush Hotel on the 25th April, 1856, when by a majority decision it had been resolved to adopt the provisions of the Local Government Act 1858, under which an elected body would take over the secular duties of the Vestry.

Voting at the public meeting, restricted to Farnham owners and ratepayers, showed little enthusiasm for change. There voted 300 for, 249 against, with 102 abstentions.

During the years of the Vestry, there had been enormous fluctuations in trade and commerce. One factor, beloved by statisticians, was one of steady growth - the population. Over a period of sixty years the population of Farnham, which included the tythings of Badshot, Runfold, Culverlands, Tilford, Runwick, Wrecclesham and The Bourne, had increased from 4,321 in 1801 to 9,278 in 1861.

Local Board 1866-1894

The first three meetings of the newly elected Local Board were held at the Bush Hotel during 1866, thereafter they transferred to the Boardroom of the aptly named Town Hall in The Borough. Early decisions of the twelve elected members were to appoint Mr Richard Mason as Clerk, at an annual salary of £25 (with the possible addition of a bonus), and to confine to one officer the duties of Surveyor, Collector and Inspector. The records of the Vestry were handed over, and with the abolition of Church Rates in 1867, the removal of the church from the management of local government in Farnham was accomplished. The civic duties of the new Board, included highways, and Lighting and watching. There is no record of the Board, as a civic authority, having any interest in organising the Venison Dinner. It was not regarded by those elected as being a Local Government function.

A report of the 1867 Venison Dinner held on Tuesday 20th August, refers back to earlier Dinners in the reign of Elizabeth and her immediate successors, as being events of considerable local importance, when wine flowed freely, and the good old Bailiffs and Burgesses, threw aside their wonten gravity as local governors, joined their townsmen, and filled their glasses at the expense of the rates, Years later, under the Stuart dynasty, sack was in great request on such occasions. The courteous host of the Bush was paid a considerable sum for this vivifying liquor, which was sold at 12d (5p) a quart at that period.

This tale of conspicuous consumption at public expense, was preceded by a sobering event which occurred at the petty sessions, when a Mary Keney, who said she came from Birmingham, was charged with stealing cabbages from a garden at Heath End, in the occupation of William James. The prisoner was seen in the garden by a witness named Joseph Gregory. Perceiving she was being watched, the woman dropped the cabbages and left the garden. She was shortly apprehended by P.C. Smith. (The Surrey Police force had been established in 1851). The prisoner was sentenced to 21 days hard labour.

Much more fortunate were the guests at the annual Tradesman's Dinner, at the Bush that year; the Bishop sending a fine buck. It seems that the generous gesture of donating a buck was not confined to the Venison Dinner. Mr J.Knight, brewer and ground landlord of the Bush, was Chairman, and Mr Barrett, also a brewer was Vice-chairman.

1867 was a black year for hops, ranking with 1840. The result was lower wage rates, which in turn led to strikes. One hop grower paid 3d a bushel for poor land and 4d a bushel for good land. The pickers rebelled, but eventually reached agreement with the growers.This harvest was sold at Weyhill Fair for £9.10s to £11 a cwt, with samples of well-cured hops reaching £12 to £13.10s a cwt. But producing costs were high, and the future of the hop industry uncertain. The growers had petitioned parliament successfully against the duty imposed on hops and now turned their attention to obtaining a reduction in the level of tythe payable. They submitted costs to parliament of 1 year and 2 years growing but on this occasion although their efforts were unsuccessful, their arguments were prophetic.

The year was also a black one for those unfortunate enough to be inmates of the Farnham Workhouse. In 1834 the care of the poor had been removed from the Vestry, and vested in the Guardians of the Poor. Boards were established with members nominated at public meetings. The deliberations of the Board reflected the official view that life in the workhouse should be less attractive than employment. There may have been occasions when, during a time of widespread poverty, the spirit of the Act would have appeared to have been applied too effectively, with a resultant perceived increase in the degree of suffering. It was perhaps inevitable that the workhouse at Farnham would attract official attention and criticism.

In 1847 the premises had been enlarged to allow for the number of inmates to be increased to 314. Whether from inadequate finance or indifferent staffing, there was a sharp deterioration in standards, to the point where there were official complaints. As a result, an investigation followed, and a report was prepared for The Lancet by Dr Joshua H.Stallard and Dr Francis E.Anstie: "A report on the State and Management of the Workhouse of the Union".The squalid conditions are described in detail, reaching the conclusion: "What can we say - what can any reasonable person say - of the Farnham Workhouse, but this: That the existence of such places is a reproach to England. - a scandal and a curse to a country which calls itself civilised and christian" The conclusions contained in the report were contested vigorously.

Other matters were now occupying the thoughts of residents. The railway had come to Farnham. The line from Guildford had opened in 1849, and the line to Alton in 1852. The line from Farnham to Aldershot and Brookwood would not open until 1870.

The road system was inadequate to meet the growing needs of modern transport. A new road to the station was proposed, thereby setting in motion Farnham's first highway petition. Headed "Road Protest" and dated 23rd November, 1868, it was addressed to the Chairman and Members of the Farnham Local Board.

"The undersigned being property and ratepayers within the district of the Local Board, hear with much regret that you have under consideration a proposal to make a new road from East Street to the railway station, and charge the rates with the cost thereof, which of necessity must amount to a very large sum of money. At the same time we are aware that the present approach to the railway station requires improvement, which we believe can be effected at a much less cost, and without interfering with existing interests, by continuing the present road from Gostrey Gate across the meadows and connecting with the public footpath from East Street whereas the proposal under your consideration would only benefit a very inconsiderable portion of the District, and is calculated to injure property and trade in some parts of the town, particularly Downing Street.

Under these circumstances we are of the opinion that the Ratepayers ought not to be called upon to bear such an expense as a cost of a road from East Street, especially when we remember that you have lately before you proposals for executing a very costly public work: we therefore beg to enter our protest against it, which we do with the more confidence understanding the members of your Board are very equally divided on the subject and we trust that you will take our suggestions into your serious consideration.

We are, Gentlemen,

Your obedient Servants. Some 215 signaturesures were attached. The petition failed.

By 1890 the new road works had been completed, at a total cost of £2,312.00. Approaches to property owners to purchase the necessary land had been received favourably, probably due to the benefits accruing to them of unexpectedly obtaining frontages onto the new highway.

Concern over the future of the local hop industry, which had been central to the prosperity of the town, did not abate. The emerging superiority of the Kent hop grounds as they expanded their markets was having an increasing impact upon the local economy. It was not surprising that visits to Kent by local growers to investigate their methods resulted. In 1869 Messrs Ellis, Hammond, Foster and Goodman, all large growers, visited Kent to evaluate the beneficial effects of a new system of syringing the hop bines with a preparation of tobacco juice and other ingredients. They returned to Farnham and experimented themselves, and declared the results to be satisfactory. One of the growers, Mr Hammond reported subsequently that 'on portions of his ground which have not been thus treated, the bine does not give promise of a crop of more than 1 cwt, or $1\frac{1}{2}$ cwt per acre; while, on some of the surrounding grounds, in which the bines were well syringed when in a filthy condition, the estimate reaches 8 cwt to 10 cwt, and on one ground as high as 12cwt to the acre. The total cost of twice syringing, including labour, is put down at from 53s to 54s per acre.'

The duties and powers of the Bishops had been under review for a number of years. The Ecclesiastical Commissioners appointed in 1836 to report upon the re-arrangement of the various dioceses, curtailed the Bishop of Winchester's income to £3,600. Later, in 1863 and 1890 they were specifically empowered to sell manorial property. But 1869 was the most significant year, when the ancient jurisdiction of the Bishop transferred to the Ecclesiastical Commission. Amongst the changes wrought were to have the Court Leet merged with the Court Baron, and thenceforth to be held once instead of twice annually, before a deputy Steward of the Commissioners. Bishop Charles Sumner remained in occupation of Farnham Castle and magnanimously continued to provide a buck annually to the Venison Dinner. His successor, Samuel Wilberforce, never resided at the Castle as Charles Sumner remained there until his death in 1874. On the 18th August, 1873, about fifty gentlemen assembled at the Bush Hotel to partake of the usual dinner of a recherché description, under the fastidious eye of Mr Bromley. The table decorations were provided by the Misses Bromley who were congratulated on the taste displayed in their arrangement. Mr James Knight was Chairman, with Mr Lorimer, Vice-Chairman. Following grace by the Archdeacon, the customary loyal toasts, and the singing of the National Anthem and "God bless the Prince of Wales", the speeches began.

The Rev. J.Sumner, (Charles Sumner's son) in proposing "The Army, Navy, and Reserve Forces" praised the efficiency of the men of the army, as exhibited in the autumn manoeuvres which had taken place during the past few years. Referring to the navy, he had the good fortune to be present at Portsmouth at the review in honour of the Shah (of Persia) and, if it did nothing else, it brought out a display of navel power that could not be equalled anywhere else in the world (applause). He spoke highly of the volunteers, whose reviews at Brighton he had witnessed and believed that so long as they possessed such a force, with the spirit they manifested, this country would have nothing to fear from foreign foes (cheers).

He coupled the toast with Dr. Lorimer, the surgeon to the Farnham corps (Cheers).

The Chairman in response regretted the absence of any officer of the army. (It was customary for two Officers from Aldershot to attend and respond to the toast.) The army was presently in a stage of transition and there was a great deal of complaining among the members of the force. He had no doubt that matters would prove satisfactory, and that the army would be put in a better position than ever it was before (hear,hear). From his knowledge of the navy, he was convinced that now, as of yore, "Brittania ruled the waves" (Loud cheers). The Volunteers had seen a diminution of numbers, but he was glad to say that the number of efficients had increased (cheers), and he was glad to say that in the Farnham corps most of them were efficient (hear,hear). The best evidence of their efficiency was to be found in the fact that the Government accorded them a contribution toward their maintenance (applause).

Dr Shepherd who had served in the crimea also responded . He referred to the great cry in certain quarters for retrenchment, and although he was not an advocate for extravagance, he thought things had come to a pretty pass when the offices of Prime Minister and Chancellor of the Exchequer, were combined in one and the same person (hear,hear).

There followed a song by Mr Moody - "My Old Friend John." The Chairman then proposed the health of one who had been known in Farnham for years and years, only to be loved and respected by everyone from their hearts - it was "our Bishop" (loud cheers). He called him "our Bishop" because they all looked upon Bishop Sumner as their Bishop. (Bishop Charles Sumner retired in 1869 but continued to reside at the Castle until his death in 1874. His successor, Bishop Samuel Wilberforce was killed in 1873 while hunting with Lord Granville, first cousin to Bishop Sumner) For many years Bishop Sumner had given them a buck for their annual dinner, and for a long time that dinner had been associated with hops - the staple commodity of the town and called the "hop betting dinner," because, according to the register, bets were made as to the amount of duty on the hops for the year, though those bets were chiefly confined to new hats (hear, hear and laughter), but as time rolled on this had been abolished and many familiar faces had ceased to attend. The Bishop was ever ready to support any charity, and to promote every good work; and if any improvement were to be carried out in the neighbourhood they always sought for, and obtained, the Bishop's assistance. No matter what was the object, so long as it was good, whether for the sanitary improvement, or for the moral and social benefit of the town, the Bishop had always come forward with open handed generosity (applause). He was sure that if the Bishop could be present at this town dinner, not a political dinner, (here we see one of the many references to the strictly non-political nature of the event) it would gladden his heart to see them enjoying his venison (applause).

The Rev.J.Sumner expressed his thanks for the cordial reception given to his father's health. Referring to the allusion made by the Chairman to his father's support of charitable objects, he said it was an implicit belief of his father that it was the duty of those who had the means, to help those who were not so fortunate; he believed in the luxury of doing good, in rejoicing with those who rejoiced, and in an ernest endeavour to alleviate the sufferings of those who were in sorrow (applause). The Chairman said that this was formerly a betting dinner, but he could not help thinking that this was a better (hear,hear). Time passed on and with it old customs passed away. The time was when Bishops of Winchester had bucks sent to them from Witchwood Forest, in Staffordshire, and similar contributions from the New Forest in Hampshire.

A subsequent toast was to "The Members for the Western Division". Parliament had been dissolved pending a General Election. Two of the candidates, Messrs Steere and Cubitt were present; Mr Cubitt in responding said that "a dinner like this was neither the occasion for a long speech nor for a political speech. It was not the occasion for a long speech, because that would be very discordant in a social gathering of this kind. They would allow also, that as members of Parliament who had only just been relieved from their work, they would require some rest; also that it would be out of place to introduce any controversial or political topics at such a meeting (hear,hear)". Mr Lee Steere was also heartily received. "He was not going to make a political speech either, as this was not the place for it (hear,hear)". The speeches and songs continued well into the night. The 1874 Dinner was suspended out of respect to Bishop Sumner who died that year. He was held in such high regard that the church of St. James, East Street, was built as a memorial to him at a cost of £4,000.

On the succession of Bishop Edward Harold Browne (1873-1890), the important question of the future occupation of the Castle arose. The Castle provided a palatial residence, one of the finest in Southern England, and a visible confirmation of the ancient and historic link between Farnham and the See of Winchester. Against this had to be balanced the enormous financial strain upon the incumbent Bishop, of maintaining the Castle in a suitable state of presentation. Bishop Browne said that the burden led to impoverishment, as his official income was totally inadequate.

After due consideration, he resolved to stay. His decision was supported by the Archbishop of Canterbury who wrote: "I am glad to hear that you have decided to keep Farnham. I am sure it is an evil to break the old ties of association, which are a help to all of us in our works." The role, and influence, of the Bishops of Winchester in the affairs of Farnham was not yet to be further reduced.

The Dinner resumed in 1875 when both Members of Parliament were present, having been re-elected. Mr James Knight took the chair, supported by Mr Cubitt, M.P., Mr Lee Steere, M.P., Rev Philip Hoaste, Rector of Farnham, Rev. Barrington Gore Browne, (son of the new Bishop) together with a large attendance. This would mean about sixty.

Unable to be present himself, the Bishop had sent a splendid buck. In proposing the toast "The Health of the Bishop of Winchester and the Clergy of the Diocese", the Chairman made reference to the origins of the dinner. He believed "it was first established as a betting dinner, and the Archbishop of Canterbury used to send a representative; he did not know whether for the purpose of making bets, or to know what way Kent people would be able to do a little better as regarding their price of hops (laughter). The new Bishop was unknown to most of them, but the buck they had partaken of was a very happy introduction. He was sure it was the wish of all of them that the Bishop would live at Farnham Castle for many years, and that he might continue to feel justified in presenting them with this annual buck. He added that Bishop Browne was a man of great literary attainments, and when he came amongst them he would claim their admiration (cheers)".

The Rev Hoaste having remarked that "it was a great duty to preserve the church for the children who came after us", continued, that he knew "there were in the world people stern and very hard, who looked upon any social gathering like the present as a great crime. He did not look on these friendly gatherings in that way (cheers). He had heard several people talking about this dinner, and they had all said it had done a great deal of good (applause). It perhaps sometimes got rid of a very unpleasant thing called 'misunderstanding' (hear,hear). He had known such occasions alter opinions about people, and someone would sit opposite to somebody else, and say to his friend next day, "Well, do you know I sat opposite Mr So-and So at dinner today, and I don't think he is half such a bad fellow after all" (cheers). He hoped the venison dinner would continue as an institution, and that there always might be such a good company there as they saw tonight. He was sure if they were pleased to see the clergy there, the clergy would be glad to be amongst them (applause)".

Both M.P.s spoke briefly. Mr Cubitt, who on rising was loudly cheered, said he had assured the Vice-Chairman when accepting the invitation, that he had no idea of attempting to turn the meeting into a political demonstration (hear,hear). He had one fear, and it was in coming down tonight he might be supposed to be playing truant, but he was relieved to find that the House of Commons was not to meet that evening, as there was no business on the paper. He wished to speak on the passing session without touching on controversial subjects. The statute book would be one of the thickest on record. Many of the Acts would give satisfaction. The Public Health Act, for instance, would lighten the labours of the Chairman of the Farnham Union (who was sitting near him). There were one or two measures affecting the social condition of the people, which without party feeling they could regard with pleasure. Amongst these were the Chancellor of the Exchequer's Friendly Societies Act, the Home Secretary's Masters and Workmen's Act, and the Artizens Dwellings Act (cheers). Mr Lee Steere was equally well received. He was now restored to health, and had great pleasure in meeting them there tonight. He rather suspected that one of the reasons they invited their Members to the venison dinner, knowing they had no right to speak on political subjects, was to see whether they were living members or not (laughter).

Other toasts were "The Army, Navy and Reserve Forces", "The Town and Trade of Aldershot", "The Press", "The Health of the Vice-Chairman", "The Visitors", "The Houses of Lords and Commons", and "The Ladies". The last could easily have been re-titled "Absent Ladies", as the dinner remained strictly male. As usual, the company was liberally entertained with songs. These included: "God Bless the Prince of Wales", "Kathleen", "The Lark", "Good News from Home", "Nancy is my Wife", "The British Lion", "The Village Blacksmith", "Stirrup Cup". The proceedings concluded with an appreciation of the committee for making the arrangements so successfully, viz: Messrs Aylwin, Beale, Burch, D.Goddard, Goujon, Hewitt, John Knight, Matthews, Moody, Nash, John Nichols, Vine and Woodbine.

The inclusion of the definition "Reserve Forces", in the toast to the Army and Navy merits an explanation. The Farnham Voluntary Infantry was formed in the early 1800's. Following a decision in 1859 to form Volunteer Forces nationally, a meeting was held at the Bush Hotel in May 1860 when it was agreed to form the 3rd Admin. Battn., 18th Surrey Rifle Volunteers. Two officers were chosen under Major Owen Ward. Officers were generally chosen in accordance with social rank. Thus the occupier of the Manor House, would expect to become the Colonel. An amusing story is told of an occasion when a new company assembled to choose their officers. It was agreed that those wishing to become officers would leave the room, while those remaining would make the decisions. All left except three. Upon returning they found that the three had chosen themselves - Major, Captain and Lieutenant!

The menu for 1877 more than adequately illustrates the apt description of 'recherché' to describe the feast 'worthy of the occasion', prepared by Mr Bromley. In that year only 5 or 6 bucks had been killed. The Bishop had given express orders that one should be sent to the venison feast. The assembled company delighted in partaking of the following:

Soup: Mock turtle, juillieme, ox tail.

Fish: Salmon & lobster sauce, fried soles, turbot & hollandaise sauce, fried whiting.
Entreés: Lamb cutlets, fricassee of chicken, sweetbreads, kidneys.
Removes: Haunches of venison, roast lamb, roast & boiled chicken, ham, tongue, ducks & peas.
Sweets: Curates pudding, tarts, jellies, blancmanges, etc. etc.
Dessert.

One cannot help but make a contrast with the soup kitchen which was a feature of Church Lane each December, for a number of years. It was organised by a committee whose treasurer and hon. secretary was John Darvill. In 1875 it opened on the 14th December and closed on the 28th January, 1876, 911 gallons of soup having been dispensed. The poor were given free tickets which were purchased by benefactors. Subscribers of 2s 6d or more in proportion had the privilege of giving one or more tickets. Subscriptions received that year totalled £86.12.11. leaving a balance in hand of £9. 0s.9½d.

Trade at Weyhill fair was now in serious decline. In 1887, a petition signed by London merchants, complained that the manner in which their trade was conducted was tedious. This petition was considered at a meeting of the Farnham & Country Hop Planters, held at the Town Hall on Thursday, 4th October, 1888. The result was a decision to limit the fair to 2 days - October 12th & 13th.

A report on hop prospects dated 5th September, 1891 mentions the rough winds with heavy showers which resulted in damage to the crop, especially where the poles were rotted, but where sound and firmly in the ground, they had withstood the gales well. Should there be sun to bring the hop on, the crop should be a good one. In many grounds, a heavy one. Although from mould and other causes there would no doubt be some inferior samples. The report makes particular mention of Firgrove, Weydon Hill and Weybourne, all important locations having good crops. "Coming from Frensham, down the Firgrove Hill, the view of the gardens is a beautiful one. Weydon Hill running beside the line and reaching the borders of the town, presents an equally pretty sight, and at Weybourne, beside the highway down by the running stream, for a distance of quite half-a-mile, the crops look very beautiful."

Photography had become established by 1891, when a photograph was taken of the tables before dinner commenced; the tables having been 'decorated with great taste and skill'.

The Local Board continued to grapple with the perceived problems affecting the town at the time. Dissatisfaction with the London & South Western Railway company was intense. In September 1892 a petition was sent to the Railway Company complaining of the lack of a waiting room, and of the delays caused by the closing of the level crossing gates. The principal signatories were A.W.Winter (Farnham Castle), R.H.Combe (Frensham) and Geo Trimmer (Farnham) supported by some 250 other objectors. Periods of activity followed, during which the Directors considered their options. They argued that the level crossing objection

*A watercolour of Castle Street in the 1880's.
Note the Nelson Arms and the public water pump.*

'Local 'hoppers' during the 1890's. It was usual for families and friends to form small working groups.'

had to be resolved in advance of any proposals for a waiting room. The stage was now set for lengthy negotiations, which were not to be resolved before the dissolution of the Local Board.

For a number of years records had been kept of the distribution of venison following the two annual culls. Recipients were mostly prelates of the church, army officers and local dignatories.

One intriguing entry for November 1894, refers to a doe weighing 50lbs to Nobody's Friends Hotel, Metropole. The name may have derived from cynical introspection, but they did, at least, have a friend in the Bishop!

The 1894 dinner held at the Bush on Thursday, 9th August is recorded as being the 110th anniversary dinner. The strict adherence to the numbering of the dinners suggests the great importance the professional people and traders of the town attached to their close personal relationship with the incumbent bishop. This view was enhanced by the guest of honour, Bishop Anthony Wilson Thorold (1890-1895) who, as Chairman, responded to the toast of the evening,"Health to the Donor of the Buck," stated that the venison dinner started in the days of Bishop Brownlow North. Continuing in a humorous vein, he added: "They knew that two processes went on. The people of Farnham had Bishop North's buck, and took one as their own". It gave him great pleasure to be among the townspeople . He did not want them to feel that he was some quaint person living at the top of the hill, but he was one of themselves, - a neighbour, a fellow townsman, and certainly, a ratepayer. The trees and the deer in the Park did not belong to him. He was only in trust for Farnham Park, not even perhaps for his life. The Bishop encouraged the use of the park by cricketers, and generally took profound interest in local matters, particularly education.

The organising committee of the dinner, which from time to time included Churchwardens and members of the various Boards, was free to continue to organise the dinners on behalf of the church and the tradesmen of the town.

Over the next fifty years, events were to change dramatically, as local government expanded and came under increasing political control.

With the government seeking an administrative structure to provide comprehensive links between government departments and small authorities it was decided to create a tier of County Councils covering the whole country. There were the predictable objections from the larger authorities, with the result that a compromise was reached. The 1888 Act was passed which exempted those authorities with populations of more than 50,000. These would become County Boroughs, with the powers of a County Council plus those of a Borough. The plight of smaller authorities was settled by the 1894 Local Government Act, which, despite a stormy passage and over 800 amendments was passed on March 5, 1894. The Act set up Urban and Rural District Councils. The Local Board was dissolved on the 31st December, 1894.

Farnham Urban District Council
1895-1974

On the Ist January, 1895 the Farnham Urban District Council came into existence, and held its first meeting in the Council Room of the Town Hall, with its 12 elected members. Mr D. Goddard became the first chairman. Other members were: Messrs Kingham, Eggar, Coleman, Bide, Bentall, Ransom, Fry, Kempson, Trimmer, Williams and Dr Hayes. Continuity was assured as the first four had been elected members of the Local Government Board. The number of members was later extended temporarily to 24. as parts of the Parish of Farnham Rural were merged with the Urban District, but was subsequently reduced to 21.

The Venison Dinners continued; sometimes described as "Consecutive," sometimes as "Anniversary", thereby leading to further confusion as to the precise number of years the dinner has been held, and as a consequence, the precise date of origin. Suffice to say that the numbering, together with the statements of various Bishops and other speakers at the dinners, fixes it at 1784. Hop betting was now a diversity of bygone years, never to be resurrected. The Hampshire Chronicle reporting in 1895 on the sharply declining hop market stated that, 'by the 19th October, only about 400 pockets of hops pitched that year, so the Weyhill Fair soon to be a thing of the past.' This prediction was vindicated as trade continued to fall. The fair became defunct in the 1920's and this 'Greatest Fair in the Kingdom' finally closed in 1959.

With the removal of betting from the dinner, there was now no compelling need for it to be held in August. Until the outbreak of World War 1, the most favoured month would be October, but occasionally in September and November.

In 1899, on the 5th October, described as the 115th anniversary dinner, again at the Bush Hotel, the new proprietor Thomas H. J.Bubb supplied a truly recherché repast. Among the company of over sixty, were Mr E.Kempson, (Chairman), Mr F.Hart, (Vice- Chairman), the Rev. Thory Gage Gardiner, (Rector), The Rev. S. Priestley, (Headmaster, Farnham Grammar School), Col. Maillard, Major Hillkirk, Dr Lorrimer, Dr G.Brown, Messrs C.Gould, QC.,JP., E.Crundwell, R.G.Trimmer, J.A.Eggar, S.Bide, A.Simmonds, (Superintendent of Police), G.Elphick, D.Kingham, A.E.Mason, W. Tiley, G.Heath, J.Lock, and C.Borelli.

Matters of national importance figured prominently in the speeches. The Chairman gave the loyal toast, and went on to refer to the crisis in the Transvaal, he said "it must be a great source of regret to her Majesty, that the closing years of her reign should be marked once more with bloodshed and warfare, but she would be comforted by the knowledge that she had the united and undying affection of her people, wherever they might be (applause)".

The Vice-Chairman in proposing the toast "The Army, Navy and

Reserve Forces," said that "at the present time they were all interested in the movements of our soldiers, who would ever give a good account of themselves (applause)". Colonel Maillard and Major Hillkirk responded, the former being of the opinion that although the Navy was somewhat overshadowed by the Army at that time, they must not forget the role the Navy had played in the past as a very potent factor in the solution of complications, which had at times unhappily arisen. All eyes were on the army; our soldiers had a tough time ahead of them. They had a competent commander in Sir Redvers Bullers, who possessed an intimate knowledge of the country (i.e. South Africa). (The inclusion of 'Reserve Forces' in the toast was to remain unchanged until the early 1900's, when it became 'His Majesty's Forces', or 'His Majesty's Imperial Forces'. The Rifle Volunteers had been re-organised into the 2nd Volunteer battn (Royal West Surrey Regt) in 1880, and in 1883 had become the 2nd Volunteer Battn "The Queens" (Royal West Surrey Regt) E Company. Parades were held at the Drill Hall, Bear Lane. The battalion had a strength of about 100)

The Chairman gave "The Bishop of Winchester". He was reminded that this was the 115th occasion that his Lordship or his predecessors had sent a fat buck to the host of the Bush Hotel, and that was quite sufficient in his mind to commend his Lordship (Dr Randall Davidson. 1895-1903) to the feelings and affections of the people of Farnham. Whether they took him as a bishop or as a man he was one of the most charming men that they could possibly meet with (applause).

Mr A.W.Chapman, JP., in submitting the toast "The Town and Trade of Farnham," paid tribute to the management of the town, but hoped for more progress. For instance, by prevailing upon the South Western Railway Company to provide a better station and better services, Farnham might be a still more attractive place if those improvements could be carried out. He was convinced it would become a larger residential neighbourhood, and he expressed a hope that it might increase by leaps and bounds. Mr Kingham, in responding, said that it was twelve years since he had first ventilated the grievance, and it still remained unredressed.

He believed that within the last forty years the trade of the town had enlarged tenfold, and yet the accommodation for passengers was little better than it was forty years ago. On the Urban Council they knew no party, they carefully guarded the interests of the ratepayers, and had effected some improvements. They endeavoured to look ahead, as was evidenced by the erection of the Isolation Hospital, in Weydon Lane.

The by now standard toasts followed, but with a reduction in the number of musical interludes.

The comments by Mr Chapman reflected the degree of concern about the inadequate facilities provided at the railway station. An attempt by the Council to resolve the matter by sending a petition to the Board of Trade ended in failure. The Board had no powers to intervene, and took no action. Meanwhile, mindful of the constant traffic congestion at Station Hill, and anxious to provide a solution, the Railway Company's engineer had produced a scheme to construct a new bridge, but not on the site of the level crossing. A new loop road would be constructed. It would leave Station Hill to a new bridge 150 yards to the east of the level crossing and exit opposite the Waverley Arms. Two houses would be demolished and the crossing removed.

In March 1897 with the U.D.C. opposing the scheme, the Railway Directors set out their case. The local authority had petitioned to have improvements carried out, and the company was now responding. Two hurdles had to be cleared; parliamentary powers would have to be obtained to close the level crossing, and the necessary land would have to be acquired. Accordingly, the Company would proceed to have a Bill placed before parliament, provided the Council put the Railway Company in possession of the required land and buildings. Again, there was public outrage. At a public meeting held at the Corn Exchange on the 12th February, 1897, about 100 people attended and resolved : 'That the ratepayers were opposed to the proposals, that ratepayers money should not be used to advance the scheme, and that the Council lodge a petition in opposition.' Also, there were questions over apparent recent purchases of strategically placed land by certain councillors. The matter became closed when the council resolved not to proceed with the acquisition of the necessary land, and to oppose formally the proposed enabling Bill. The company replied, stating that it was now too costly to continue, and pointed out, with justification, that the council had started the matter by sending a petition, and concluded it by sending another. There followed attempts to persuade the Railway Company to construct a subway. These received a polite but firm rejection.

This was not the only matter having commercial undertones occupying the attention of the council at that time. The Farnham Gas Company, having received many requests to supply gas outside their legal area of operation, was in process of presenting a Draft Provisional Order to parliament to allow it to 'construct, maintain and continue' a gas supply to both parishes of Farnham Urban and Farnham Rural. To this end it had gone into voluntary liquidation and immediately reformed with an increased capital of £8,000.

The Council opposed the proposals vigorously, and offered to purchase the company for the sum of £20,000, and threatened the Gas Company with a Compulsory Purchase procedure in the event of their offer being refused.

The Gas Company did refuse. Following a costly legal battle the Council's objection was not upheld. During the course of lengthy legal cross-examination, the Secretary for the Gas Company was asked whether all shareholders had been informed of the Council's offer. He stated that they had, and that all but one had rejected the offer. It appeared that the sole shareholder who supported the Council, was himself a councillor.

The strictly apolitical nature of the dinner was emphasised again at the 116th, held on the 18th August, 1900, with a record attendance of 84. One of the two principal speakers was the Rt Hon. St.J.Brodrick MP. Secretary of State for War, 1900-1903 who was in the Chair, and was later to become Lord Midleton. The other principal speaker was his political opponent, Mr A.W.Chapman, JP., the Liberal candidate. On the whole the speakers skilfully avoided overstepping the bounds of propriety by mentioning anything remotely savouring of politics, but when one of them appeared likely to transgress when responding to the toast "Her Majesty's Forces", he was promptly met with cries of 'no politics'.

As Secretary of State for War, St John Brodrick had received universal criticism in the press. At the 1902 Dinner, when responding to the toast 'Her Majesty's Ministers', he took the opportunity to hit back. He referred to comments made to him by Sir Michael Hicks-Baach, Chancellor of the Exchequer, and said that 'the army would never be efficient unless removed from all outside influences, which now interfere with the management of the army, with the solutions for appointments and promotions - interferences which would never be tolerated at any other organised department of the civil service. It was not a party question. If it were he would not have ventured upon anything of the kind that night. If the administration of the army and the promotions and appointments were made the subject of favouritism, then indeed we must despair. It was Sir Michael who had said to him - 'war office is in need of reform.' His (Sir Michaels)duty was to reduce the national expenditure.

He spoke of the discharge of nearly 4,000 men in 4 months. A large number for the labour market of the country to absorb. One thing the government could do, was to take care of the men who served their country. It was St John Brodrick who was 'credited', but according to him 'discredited' with the introduction of the Brodrick hat to the army. It was a round hat with a large flat top, and was universally disliked. He was later to write that he left all questions of military dress to the military authorities. A cap of this fashion was first designed and approved for a regiment of foot guards months before he had come to the War Office. In 1901 the military authorities had decided to make this cap universal to the army. He had been informed that it had been necessary for this cap to supersede the 'Field Service Cap', on military grounds. The cap was so unpopular that it was quietly discontinued.

That same year (1902) the new offices for the Urban District Council were built in South Street. The rooms at the Town Hall buildings were vacated. In 1903 the Council proudly announced that the opening ceremony would be carried out by the Archbishop of Canterbury, Bishop Randall Davidson. Perfectly true. He had a special relationship with Farnham, as until his recent promotion he had resided at the Castle as the Bishop of Winchester, which was fifth in rank among the prelates of the Church of England. He was only too pleased to return to his beloved Farnham. He had been succeeded by Bishop Herbert Edward Ryle (1903-1911).

At the 1903 Dinner, with the Bishop of Winchester presiding, General Sir John French gave a tribute to the Secretary of State for War, stating that 'Brodrick had grappled successfully with the great military problems of the day'. The Vice-Chairman, Earnest Jackson, in proposing 'The Success of the Venison Dinner' spoke of Bishop Brownlow North, 199 years ago, discovering his deer herd diminishing - they were not multiplying as orthodox ecclesiastical deer should, so he made a pact. In consequence of enquiries, he had found the inhabitants of Farnham were making away with fat bucks. Hence the annual donation of a fat buck to the town. For over 50 or 60 years the Dinner had been connected with hop betting. He was informed that the citizens of Farnham were not now waging war on hops, but preferred something that travelled a little faster. This was the last occasion the Dinner would be held at the Bush Hotel. (Not entirely correct; they would be held at the Bush for another two years). Their host had reached the conclusion that sleeping was more profitable than dining. (The Assembly Room was subsequently converted into bedrooms). Of one thing he was certain. If it would please his Lordship to continue his hospitality, and continue to give a fat buck each year to the town, the citizens would make arrangements to meet and dine together in some other room.

The kind of room he had in mind would not be found in the Farnham Workhouse. The unfortunates who were sent there faced a very different lifestyle, as the following cases heard at Farnham Police Court in September 1903 illustrate:

Ashamed of Clothes

Thomas Beaver was charged with destroying his clothes while an inmate of the casual ward. Prisoner said the clothes he wore were so bad that he was ashamed to go home in them. He was sent to prison for 14 days.

A Lazy Casual

Before Captain Bacon (in the chair) and Mr W.T.Coleman, George Roberts was charged with refusing to work while an inmate of the casual ward on August 21st. He pleaded guilty. Kemp, the porter gave evidence. The prisoner was sent to gaol for 14 days hard labour.

It was customary for the press to receive invitations to the Venison Dinner each year. In 1905 it appears that no invitation was issued, with the result that the following letter appeared in the Surrey & Hants News dated 14th October :

"Surely it was a mistake not to invite the press to the Venison Dinner last week, for general interest is locally felt in this function and the proceedings this year were quite as worthy of publication as in times gone by. It is most unusual in this country for newspaper men to walk furtively into a dining room after the cloth has been removed, the universal custom being to invite the members of the fourth estate to dine with the other welcome guests at every banquet - Let us another year, pay a little more for our tickets if such a course be necessary to provide the needed funds, so that press invitations may be issued and the time honoured venison feast conducted with that dignity and importance which the speeches usually justify, and in accordance with the position and respect due to the ancient town of Farnham. I am not a member of the committee, but can with truth, subscribe myself "ONE WHO WAS THERE"."

There is no doubt that the organising committee was beset with difficulties. The loss of the Assembly Room at the Bush Hotel meant that, for the 1906 dinner, they needed to find another attractive room in the town centre capable of seating in excess of 100, with any monetary loss being met by themselves. Yet they still had the support of the Bishop of Winchester, who would continue to provide a fat buck, and, if requested, preside over the proceedings (He did in fact supply one young buck and two haunches). At this point there was a strong possibility that the dinner would be abandoned. A meeting of committee members was held to consider their options. Opinions were expressed that the dinner should be held in a larger room than could be obtained at the Bush, (it appeared that the only room available would hold only 48) and on a lesser expensive scale than in the past, so as to enable more people to attend, but against this was the fact that if the dinner took place in such a building as the Corn Exchange, a sufficient number of persons would not purchase tickets to make it a financial success. One of those present was Mr J.A.Eggar, a well-respected businessman who was also a local councillor. He offered to arrange a public meeting to obtain a wider opinion. The meeting was held, when it was decided that future dinners would be preceded by a 'Public Meeting' convened by the Chairman of the U.D.C. at which an organising committee would be elected for the ensuing year. This arrangement had obvious advantages for the organising committee. There would be an annual public meeting to

'This little family group is working in the hop fields off what is now Manks Walk, Farnham. At the time, about 1903, the area was known as The Hollows, and the hops, which belonged to the Andersons of Waverley Abbey House are seen growing on poles. Stringing had yet to be introduced.

precede each dinner, at which the organising committee would be appointed, thereby ensuring the independent nature of the function. An additional benefit would be the privilege of holding their meetings in the Council Chamber. Equally of importance, was the possibility of the Council providing assistance with labour to assist in setting out the tables in the Corn Exchange, and to provide flowers to mollify the stark appearance of the hall. The 1906 dinner would, after all, take place.

That dinner was noteworthy in that it was the first to be held at the Corn Exchange, in The Borough. The occupations of those attending were undergoing significant changes. The growing of hops had become a less attractive occupation. By the early 1900's it was said that over a full year, the grower would incur a loss of £2-£3 on every cwt of hops sold. Increasing competition from Kent continued to have a major impact. The result was that trade at Weyhill Fair had slumped considerably. There were fewer hop growers and maltsters, while the growth in wholesale and retail occupations was spreading. The impact of commuting potential provided by the new railway, was yet to play a part, albeit relatively small, in the need for growth in housing and transport facilities.

Prominent tradespeople continued to play an important part in the management of the town's affairs, with the venison dinner being one of the most important social events of the year, attracting good company, and, with the local press now well established, good publicity. It may have been with these factors in mind that Mr J.A, Eggar, who was now Chairman of the Council, stated at the meeting of the Finance and Labour Committee on the 3rd September,1907, that, in compliance with the decision of the previous public meeting, and with the concurrence of his colleagues he proposed to convene a public meeting for the purpose of considering and making arrangements for holding that year's Venison dinner.

Mr Eggar explained that it had been the wish of the public meeting held the year before that the Chairman of the Urban Council should, when the time came round take this action, and the Chairman had undertaken to call a public meeting accordingly. There was no dissent.

The 1907 dinner (123rd anniversary) was held on Thursday, 24th October at the Corn Exchange. About 130 people attended, which was described as probably the largest gathering in its history. Mr R.Samson decorated the hall, which was hung with national and other flags and shields, the platform having scenes representing the interior of an old Baronial Hall, emblazoned with coats of arms, including those of the diocese. Hothouse plants adorned the platform, and the tables were also decorated; the tables being placed in three rows with three across. Bishop Herbert Ryle presided, supported by W.H.Cowan M.P., the excellent dinner being served by Messrs Ranson & Sons. The venison was provided as usual by the Lord Bishop (1 picket and two legs). In proposing the toast, "Our Imperial Forces", Sir W.Hoad Treacher, said: "England was no longer the workshop of the world. Other nations were doing their best to keep out our manufactories by imposition of hostile tariffs. We still had time to arrange preferential terms with the colonies. The only way to retain our possessions was to prepare for war. The late war showed the military organisation to be defective".

General Leefe responded for the Navy. There was no tradition for a naval officer to respond.

W.H.Cowan, MP., proposing "The Town and Trade of Farnham", said that Farnham had had a strange experience. It had seen the extinction of one manufacture - that of cloth, and had survived it by the establishment of at least one other - brewing - owing to the extraordinary quality of the hops produced in the neighbourhood. Farnham now had attractions as a residential district.

Bishop Herbert Ryle, in proposing "The Venison Dinner" uttered a wish, a feint aspiration - it was in connection with the poor. "Were they in a position to act together in dealing in some satisfactory way with the problems of the poor and destitute, and the unemployed? He supposed there were schemes in the air which would be well for some of the farsighted and intelligent citizens to keep in mind and consider whether something could not be done. At present they were constantly overlapping each other in their attempts to do good, in dealing with charity. Very often it became a system of doles, which did more harm than good. If they could face the problems with the spirit of self-denial, co-operation and self-sacrifice, they would do in their little town and neighbourhood a really good deed in their generation, and they would do more good for the cause of the poor than they would in any other conceivable way" (applause).

The dinner concluded at 11.00pm with the National Anthem.

The minutiae of the dinner did not go unrecorded. Wines were by Farnham United Breweries Ltd; cigars and cigarettes by Mr J.Price, The Borough, and mineral waters by Messrs Fenn of Farnham.

Ladies were not yet invited to attend the dinner, but new legislation enabled them to be elected to a local authority. In 1907 women could stand for election, provided they were over 30 years of age. Later, in 1928, this restriction was reduced to 21.

The speeches at the dinners had covered subjects ranging from the purely domestic, to matters of national, even international importance. The Bishops and Members of Parliament always had special knowledge of current international matters and made frequent reference to them. It was not surprising that at the 1909 dinner, Bishop Ryle, who had travelled extensively on the continent made the following comments that may have puzzled some of those present, but were extremely perceptive, and sadly, remarkably apposite. In replying to "The Venison Dinner", he spoke of his recent travels. "He was sure there was no subject of such serious importance as that of national defence. He had visited Germany, towards which public attention had been drawn earlier that year. It was a great and magnificent empire, and they could learn many things of it in regard to the promotion of the arts of peace, and the wonderful way in which the Germans had extended capacities of municipal institutions.

The Germans were a peace loving nation, and they were led by a great and famous potentate. The German emperor was a man of genius, and of noble instincts. He was fond of this country and whenever he paid a visit (to Britain) he showed his sympathy with our people and with their institutions. He was, he believed, a friend of Great Britain. They had, therefore, the Great German nation desiring peace, and the great German emperor who was a friend and ally of this country. But there was always, no doubt, an element of danger where they had a great army, and a great military nation. There were always the possibilities of misunderstanding. If ever such misunderstanding approached the verge or the possibility of war we would be brought face to face with real dangers.

Personally, he did not think the people of this country understood the greatness of the dangers with which, under such possibilities, which God forbid should ever arise, we would be confronted. We in Farnham had shown an example to the rest of Surrey. Farnham's territorials were at full strength - the only one in Surrey".

Within a few years, his fears would be seen to have been well founded.

For several years the Annual Public Meeting had been held in the Council Chamber. Following one of these meetings, Mr Mardon, a Councillor, questioned the right of the committee to have the use of the Chamber. They had nowhere else to hold their meetings, and the matter subsided when Mr A.G. Mardon became the Chairman and presided over the meeting held on the Ist October, 1910. The Bishop had been invited to make the customary gift of venison and to preside at the dinner. He had replied that he would be glad to give the venison but lameness prevented him from attending, therefore someone else would have to be chairman. A committee was appointed to make the arrangements. Mr J.W.Wright, Clerk to the U.D.C. was elected the hon. secretary.

Mr Kessell moved that ladies be invited. This proposal was seconded by Mr H.Mitchell, but the amendment moved by Mr J.A.Eggar - that the proposal be adjourned until the public had had an opportunity of discussing it - was seconded, and adopted, thereby ensuring that no action was taken!

Since 1789 the Bailiff's Cup, charters and other documents handed to Bishop Brownlow North by William Shotter had languished in the Castle. Bishop Ryle who had suffered poor health for a number of years, announced that he would be leaving the Castle to take up a new position as Dean of Westminster, and would shortly be leaving Farnham. At the time it was known that the Bishop's son had recently married. The wedding present given by the Council on behalf of the citizens was a replica of the Byworth Cup, an item unlikely to have been found on their wedding list! It had the desired effect, for the Bishop soon announced that as the new authority now had town offices of their own, it was right that he should pass to them what really belonged to them. i.e. the charters and all documents and artifacts surrendered by William Shotter.

Accordingly, on the 22nd February, 1911, an historic meeting took

Stringing the Hop Gardens
This photograph illustrates graphically some of the skills and dexterity needed in the hops gardens following the introduction of the 'stringing' method.

place at the Castle. A deputation of the council, comprising E.Kempson, C. Borelli. J.W.Wright (Clerk) headed by A.G.Mardon (Chairman) met the Bishop's representatives, the Rector and Mr F.W.Speak the Bishop's secretary. The priceless relics were handed over. This was the last act by Bishop Ryle in his episcopal relationship with Farnham. After signing a form of transfer the deputation left. That evening Mr Mardon entertained Members of the Council, Officers, Mr Speak and representatives of the town, to a recherché dinner in the council chamber. The catering was by Mr Fisher of the Bush Hotel. The beribboned menu, comprising eight pages printed in red and green listed:

Oysters (native)
Soups: Clear Turtle, Cream of Chicken
Fish: Boiled Salmon, Prawn Sauce, Cucumber Salad, New Potatoes
Entrée: Sweetbreads and New Peas
Joint: Roast Saddles of Lamb, Mint Sauce, Sorbet, Kirsch
Second Course: Roast Quails and Salad
Sweets: Trifles, Macedaine of Fruits in Jelly
Savoury: Herring Roes on Toast
Dessert: Coffee

On show were the cup, charters, the various documents, and a wooden model of the old Market House made by Mr Tigwell. In proposing the toast "The Study of Local History", Mr Mardon referred to

The Great Hall in Bishop Talbot's time.
Note the portraits of former Bishops.
The opening from the gallery has since been filled in.

the Quaint Regulations their ancestors had imposed upon them by the Bailiffs and Burgesses. Residents were forbidden to blow horns or whistle in the streets or their houses after 9.00pm. Still more dreadful was another prohibition: they must not cause uproar by beating their wives after 9.00pm. Presumably, they could beat their wives before that time as much as they liked!

The toast "Past and Present Benefactors of Farnham" was given by the Rector. Included were people distinguished in history like Henry VII, who, out of gratitude to the town for the care of his little girl, endowed a chantry at the Parish Church, from which the Grammar School sprang. Bishops like those who granted the charters, and others like Henry de Blois who brought the episcopal residence to Farnham; Bishop Morley who endowed the Grammar School, and Bishops, not least Dr Ryle, the latest benefactor. There were also many charities and almshouses created by numerous local families and individuals.

"The Future of Farnham", was proposed by Mr E.Crundwell. In his opinion the town was not yet ready for the revival of the charter. The future of Farnham lay in it continuing to be a good residential district. The Byworth Cup was filled with wine and passed round. There were songs and a piano. The evening concluded with 'Auld Lang Syne' and the National Anthem. Altogether, an evening worthy of a truly historic event in the history of the town.

At that time the Wey was a salmon river. The U.D.C. was not a riparian authority, yet the elected members had, with acuity worthy of the seventeenth century Burgesses, obliged the fishmongers to give the best salmon to the Council on Good Fridays. If they had no salmon they had to give their best fish.

The public meeting to arrange the 127th dinner was presided over by Mr C.E.Borelli. The Bishop was willing to provide a buck and said that Thursday, 2nd November was a suitable date for him.

The new Bishop would preside, with Mr Borelli as Vice-Chairman. The committee was: The Rector, Messrs Aldridge, Eggar, Figg, Falkard, Kingham, German, Kempson, Mitchell, Preston, and Drs Tanner and Ealand. J.W.Wright was again appointed hon. secretary. Mr A.J.Bonnard suggested that a charge of 6/- should be made in order to obtain a more representative gathering of the townspeople, the Rector remarking that the lower the charge for dinner the more popular it would be. Decisions regarding the charge and the venue were left to the committee.

The dinner was held at the Corn Exchange on the 9th November. In the absence of Bishop Talbot (1911-1924) who was indisposed, Mr R.D.Anderson presided. Mr Borelli in replying to the toast "The Venison Dinner & the Town & Trade of Farnham" said that he had observed an almost fairy transformation of Gostrey Meadow. It had been converted from a clammy meadow into a beautiful public garden. Special reference was made to the gracious act of Bishop Ryle in restoring the Charters, the Bailiffs records, and the Byworth Cup to the town prior to his retirement. The Byworth cup was used for the loyal toast for the first time since 1770.

The dinners continued to be organised by a committee and hon. secretary elected annually at a public meeting, until the outbreak of war in 1914.

It was the custom to send fat bucks to Leadenhall Market to obtain the best prices. The deserving poor were never overlooked, as is shown by the information placed in the local press on the 26th day of August, 1914, by J.Alfred Eggar, the agent for the Bishop of Winchester. "It has been decided to sell venison in this place to families of the labouring classes. Prices: Prime pieces 9d per Ib. Second ditto 7d per Ib. Flank 6d. Scrag end 3d to 4d per Ib. Application to Mr Peerman, Keepers House, who will inform applicants when the venison is ready. It must be taken to the Keepers House and paid for at the time".

Keepers House, more usually known as The Rangers House, had been tenanted by Alfred Peerman who subsequently moved to South Africa. It is on the site of a lodge house shown on a map of about 1680 by John Sellers. Mr Peerman reminisced about the deer herd numbering 100. Stags were caught and exchanged for stags from Peper Harow Park. To catch the stags, posts were driven into the ground, corn was scattered around them, and a net was draped over the post. When the stags came for the corn, their antlers became entangled in the net. He recalled a stag being shot each year for the Venison Dinner. The Park was never a purely pleasure ground, as it was expected to make its contribution to the episcopal exchequer by providing venison and timber.

No dinners were held during the war years 1914-1918.

During the war years many Farnham families lost dear relatives on active service. Conditions in Flanders were particularly horrific with men, horses and vehicles stuck for years in stalemate and impenetrable mud. Yet just a few miles behind the lines a normal life was just possible. The Bishop's sons, Neville and Gilbert, left The Castle for active service. In the autumn of 1915 the British army decided to open a club for the troops at Poperinge. They had the inspiration to place in charge, an army chaplain, the Rev. Philip 'Tubby' Clayton. The club, situated in the abandoned house of a hop merchant, needed a name.

Suggestions such as Church House were rejected as too unimaginative. It was decided finally, against the protestations of Lt. Neville Talbot, to name the club Talbot House, in memory of his younger brother, Gilbert, who had been killed in July 1915.

The club provided fellowship, without regard to rank or creed, but in a basically Christian atmosphere. It was not an officers' club or a club for "other ranks". It was "Everyman's Club". This "homely" club soon became known by the initials T.H. which became Toc H in the language of the signallers of the day. The organisation grew, and possessed a Royal Charter and royal patronage, when a Farnham branch opened in 1922. A ritual soon developed with branches lighting a lamp for the duration of their meetings.

Local historians have failed to acknowledge the credit due to 'Tubby' Clayton as being the founder, preferring instead to claim it 'for Farnham'.

This is evidenced by referring to "A Brief History of Farnham", currently available on the internet.

The ending of the war on the 11th hour of the 11th day of the 11th month, was to be observed throughout the nation and the British Empire by a two-minute silence on Armistice Day. The observance was first held in 1920, and continued until 1938, when it was suspended at the outbreak of the Second World War.

The origin of the silence forms an interesting study. There are many claimants. One name proposed by a number of local authors is Mr A.E. Eggar of Castle Street. If this claim succeeds, it must be marked by the erection of a plaque in Castle Street, and be included in the Town Walks, for the benefit of tourists.

Unfortunately, careful research does not support this contention. Mr Eggar may have played a significant part, as he undoubtedly initiated the observance locally. But the favourite nominee, and one to whom official recognition has been given, is Sir Percy Fitzpatrick of Cape Town, South Africa. Sir Percy was an interesting, though controversial character. Arrested after the Jameson Raid he received a prison sentence, but was released by President Kruger on the promise that he would not meddle in South African politics for three years. He was noted for being the author of 'Jock of the Bushveld', and 'The Transvaal From Within'. Both his obituary in The Times, and his entry in the Dictionary of National Biography (1931-1940) state: "To him also is due the initiation of the two minutes' silence observed on Armistice Day." The official seal is given under a letter from Buckingham Palace, dated 30th January, 1930 stating that the King attributed the idea to Sir Percy.

Confirmation that there had been no change in official attribution was given at the service at the Menim Gate on 11th November 1998, to commemorate the 80th anniversary of the cessation of hostilities. The ceremony was attended by Queen Elizabeth II and King Harold V of Norway. Before the sounding of the Last Post by the firemen buglers of Ypers, the commentator stated that the two minute silence had originated in South Africa.

At a Special Meeting of the U.D.C. on the 16th September, 1919 the Clerk reported that acting on the instructions of the Chairman, he had written to the Bishop of Winchester asking whether his Lordship proposed to revive the ancient gift of a fat buck to the town, and whether in the event of the Venison dinner being revived he would preside. His Lordship had replied stating that he would be very pleased to revert to the old custom, and would be pleased to preside if a date were fixed on which he were free. It was resolved unanimously that the old custom be revived and that the committee appointed on the last occasion be re-appointed, with the addition of Messrs Atkins, Baker, and Swansborough to make the necessary arrangements. This was the first occasion that a public meeting had not been called to appoint the organising committee, and was to signal a fundamental change. From now on, it would be the Council who would make the annual decision to hold the dinner and appoint the committee.

The 1919 dinner was held at the Corn Exchange and presided over by Bishop Talbot who donated the buck. The event remained all male.

It appeared that up to 1919 the Council had kept ducks in Gostrey Meadow, the eggs being distributed among the poor. Regrettably, the Chairman of the Open Spaces Committee had introduced into the meadow, a swan, which chased the ducks, who became agitated, and ceased to lay. The swan was given priority and the ducks were soon removed, thus bringing to an abrupt conclusion a worthy enterprise that could only occur in a small caring community.

The 1920 dinner, the 131st, was presided over by Mr Ernest Jackson, who was notable for attending 29 dinners in all. Mr J.W.Swansborough, the Chairman of the U.D.C. was Vice-Chairman. References were again made of Farnham's status as a local government body. A petition had been lodged for the grant of a Charter of Incorporation. This move did not instantly receive the support of the County Council. It was not until 1926 that their objection was removed, only for another more serious objection to materialise. In 1929, a Royal Commission on Local Government laid down that a minimum population of 20,000 would normally be a condition, precedent to the submission of a Petition for a Charter. The submission was abandoned as the population of Farnham fell well below the minimum figure.

These were years of widespread unemployment and distress among the working classes, and it was decided not to hold a dinner in 1921, as it would create an unfavourable reaction. This decision was seized upon by the Rector, the Rev. J.M.C.Crum, at a Sunday observance of the anniversary of the armistice, which was attended by members and officials of the U.D.C. He made an appeal to those who would have attended the abandoned Venison Feast to give the money they would have expended, to the Unemployment Fund.

If only the 100 men who would have attended gave 10s 6d each, that would mean 50 guineas to the fund. It would show a temper toward the multitudinous social troubles of which they could not calculate the consequence. It would be a line that could be understood by those who thought others did not care. People who would say "They are ashamed to feast in public, but they feast all right in private every day".

The reference by the Rector to the Unemployment Fund, highlights the recognition over many years by the Council and the community, of the plight of those suffering distress due to war service, and poverty arising out of unemployment. The close relationship with Aldershot resulted in an understanding of the problems and hardships suffered by the families of soldiers during war service. In particular, with the difficulties faced by soldiers following demobilisation at the end of a campaign.

As a result, the Local Board had, in 1899, following a public meeting, established a fund in aid of wives and families of soldiers serving in South Africa. By 7th November, 1899 the fund had reached £200. This fund was superseded in 1914 by 'The Farnham & District War Relief

Fund'. In turn, this led to the setting up in 1922 of an annual 'Christmas Gift Fund'. The fund was administered by the Council with donations requested from the business community, who responded generously. Vouchers were distributed for either meat, groceries or coal. During the years of the depression, two butchers, Mr Ferguson and Mr Bolton, also gave their unsold meat on the Saturday evening preceding Christmas to the unemployed. The fund continued until 1992, when vouchers for £5 for married couples and £3 for single persons were distributed. It was then considered that widespread poverty no longer existed, and the small sums available would not be of real assistance to those found to be in desperate need.

There may have been other reasons for the decision to abandon the dinner in 1921. An adverse report had been received from the auditor. It appeared that there were numerous discrepancies and deficiencies in the accounts. His recommendations included employing an additional member of staff with a knowledge of accountancy. The dinner was revived in 1922, and organised by a committee appointed by the Council: Cllrs Mardon, Figg, Atkins, Borelli, and Jones. As always, they had power to co-opt.

There was immediate consternation when the Bishop announced that due to the high cost of maintaining the herd, he had been obliged to give instructions for the deer to be dispersed from the Park.

Shocked by this unforeseen disclosure of episcopal retrenchment, the council gave the matter thoughtful consideration. They would not lightly forgo future donations of a buck. Mr Mardon was to interview the Bishop in an endeavour to find a solution. As an interim measure, the Bishop suspended his instructions. A suggestion that a fund be set up to assist the Bishop with the high costs of repairing the 3 miles of fencing needed to restrain the deer from encroaching on neighbouring gardens, failed to receive public support. It became impossible to preserve the herd. Bishop Talbot re-issued his orders, as the removal of the herd had become an economic necessity.

At the council meeting held on the 4th September, 1923, it was agreed to continue to hold the ancient Venison Dinner. A Sub-Committee comprising the Chairman, Deputy Chairman, and Chairmen of the Standing Committees was appointed to make the arrangements. Lord Midleton, no longer the MP for Farnham, remained an enthusiastic and benevolent supporter of the dinner. He volunteered immediately to supply a buck from Peper Harow Park, when the supply from Farnham Park ceased. His generous offer was accepted and continued until the outbreak of World War II. Lord Midleton is worthy of special mention. Peper Harow Park had been the seat of the Lords Midleton of Cork since the early 1700's. As William St. John Brodrick, he had entered parliament at the remarkably early age of 24. He served both parliament and local government with distinction, as the following c.v. illustrates:

  M.P. for West Surrey   1880-1885
  M.P. for Guildford   1885-1906

Financial Secretary, War Office	1886-1892
Under Secretary for War	1895-1898
Privy Councillor	1897
Under Secretary, Foreign Affairs	1896-1900
Secretary for War	1900-1903
Secretary for India	1903-1905
Alderman L.C.C.	1907-1913
Made Knight of St. Patrick	1915
Member Irish Convention	1915-1916
Created an Earl	1920

The title became extinct in 1979.

(The link with Lord Middleton continued into the 1980's. The butler to the Middleton family, George Brumwell, was a Member of the Guild of Toastmasters, and frequently officiated at the Dinner. Mr Brumwell's varied background - his father had been a docker at Newcastle - led to numerous engagements as a after-dinner speaker in his own right.)

The Bishop, no longer the donor of the buck, was never again to receive the honour of presiding. This position, apart from 1925 when the Chair was taken by Lord Midleton, was to be the preserve of the Chairman of the U.D.C..

The dinner continued to be revived on an annual basis. With the extension of the franchise to women, and their right to become elected councillors, it was inevitable that in 1923, ladies would attend, and speak. Mrs Watkins had been elected to the council, and was chosen to respond to the toast 'The Ladies'. Mrs Watkins said that she was flattered to be the first woman to make a speech.

It was at this dinner that Dr Talbot announced his impending retirement, and his departure from Farnham Castle. The council expressed the sincere regret felt generally in the town, that the time had arrived for him to lay down the cares of high office, which of necessity meant the severance of the ties between the Bishop and his family, and the town. A kindly relationship had always existed, and it was appropriate that the inhabitants were invited to attend at the Corn Exchange on the 16th October to bid farewell to Dr E.S.Talbot and the Hon. Mrs Talbot. As a sign of especial friendship, and to mark his twelve eventful years among the people of Farnham, he was presented with a silver replica of the Byworth Cup.

The Bishop was unable to attend the Venison Dinner on the 25th October, but did donate a buck.

There were other significant changes taking shape in the detail of the dinner. The military connection was lessening. The toast 'Our Imperial Forces' was soon to be dropped. No longer would two senior officers from Aldershot be invited to give responses. The toasts had been reduced from the nine of the nineteenth century to four or five. The reduction in the number of toasts did not reduce the desire to orate, as there was no corresponding reduction in the length of the proceedings. Dinners would commence at 7.00pm and still continue until midnight.

The 1924 dinner resulted in a financial loss to the council, the precise amount being left blank in the council minutes. There was a predictable reaction the next year. With enthusiasm waning, the council showed little interest. The proposal to revive was lost by 6 votes to 3. This decision to abandon the dinner received further consideration at the Finance Committee where there appeared to be a consensus of opinion, that while the council did not see their way to take any action in the matter, they had no objection to, and in fact would welcome action by, any representative citizens for continuing the function. Mrs Stroud thought the speeches were boring. Could they be shorter? Mr Ranson declared that he was glad it had not been arranged because he regarded it as being one of the most boring functions in Farnham. Mr Borelli replied that it would be a pity if such an old institution were to pass away. To loud laughter, Mr Ewart suggested, 'Refer it to the Museum Committee'. It was disclosed that the dinner had rarely been a financial success, and that for many years Mr Mardon, a councillor, had met the deficiency himself. Mr Stevens proposed that it should be resurrected from time to time, and not necessarily every year. Again a vote was taken. This time four voted for continuance and three against. With this support a 'committee' went ahead. With apologies from the Lord Bishop, and Mr Samuel, the newly elected MP, coupled with the indifferent attitude of councillors, and the date chosen - 31st December - it was not surprising that only 40 attended. Lord Midleton, in proposing the principal toast, referred to the origin of the dinner, said that no town was the worse for having a tradition that kept it together.

While the tradition of the Venison Dinner would survive, another feudal relic would not. Often called "Tom Fools Court", the last Court Leet, or Baron Court, was held at the Bush Hotel in 1925. Manorial courts had been held there since the 1860's when the Ecclesiastical Commission took over the estates of the Bishop of Winchester.

At the 136th dinner held on the 9th December, 1926, Bishop Frank Theodore Woods (1924-1932) made his first, and last, attendance at the dinner. Dr H.F.Ealand observed that this was the first occasion that the Bishop of Winchester had attended as a guest. Previously he had attended as the host, and had always presided, the pièce de résistance for their repast. He regretted that the historic continuity that had existed between Farnham and the Diocese of Winchester for 800 years was to be broken. Bishop Woods in reply referred to the deer in the Park. They were tiresome, and had the habit of eating the fencing and equally palatable objects, although beautiful up to a point. It was quite clear why the deer had become tiresome. Under Cromwell the herds ran short, while under Charles II at his restoration, he replenished them from Germany. It was entirely due to their German blood that they became tiresome, and caused him to dispose of them.

He often looked at the heads of deer in his Great Hall, and wondered which of his predecessors was responsible for their destruction. There had been perhaps in days gone by, and there were at the present time sportsmen who had shot deer, and birds and so on.

There was a distinguished Bishop who belonged to the small and insignificant town of Guildford, where a hospital still bore his name, who once went shooting. Unfortunately his cross bow was rather ill aimed, and so instead of bringing down a deer, he brought down a keeper. The result was that an important commission was appointed by James I. On the commission was one of his distinguished predecessors, Bishop Andrews. The commission of 5 laymen and 5 Bishops had to decide whether the Bishop ought to be deposed from his high office, and regarded as incapable of discharging it. There was a majority of one to acquit him of any malice or ill-feeling. As the story went, the Bishop never smiled again. As a kind of penance he built the famous Abbots Hospital in High Street, Guildford. Dr Woods was the last Bishop of Winchester to be associated with Farnham.

Arthur Samuel, MP., spoke of Farnham's chances of becoming a borough. He said that this had a way of cropping up from time to time without any special solution, and with apparent loss of enthusiasm at local level. It was still going the rounds in higher echelons.

1927 was a significant year for the church in Farnham. The Winchester diocese had existed since the early 10th century. It comprised two counties: Hampshire and the Isle of Wight, plus Surrey minus the Croydon Deanery. It was now to be divided to create the new diocese of Guildford, which included the parish of Farnham.

Before the Bishop of Winchester vacated Farnham Castle, the portraits of twenty four past Bishops who had resided in Farnham since 1367 had been removed by Mrs Rupert Anderson of Waverley Abbey, and copies made by various artists, under the direction of Bertrand Priestland, RA. It is these copies which now adorn the walls of the Great Hall. The future use and occupation of the Castle became the subject of extensive debate.

It was resolved by dividing the Castle to allow the major part to be used for ecclesiastical purposes, with a separate accommodation for the Bishop. From now onward it would be the Bishop of Guildford who would attend the dinner, in his role as an honoured guest, to respond to the principal toast. Unlike the Bishop of Winchester, the Bishop of Guildford did not have an automatic seat in the House of Lords. He joined the sixteen Bishops awaiting election on the basis of seniority to fill a vacancy. The Manor of Farnham did not pass to him. That title was retained by the Commissioners, to be held in abeyance for another 59 years.

The tickets for the 1927 dinner cost ten shillings. The Bush Hotel remained the venue. The Chairman was C.E.Borelli with A.J.Figg, Vice-Chairman. The menu was more modest than those of the 19th century. It was not 'sumptuous', or 'recherché' but with an attendance of only 55, it was an evening to be enjoyed by councillors, their wives and husbands, the representatives of surrounding local authorities and a few officers and friends. Guests would have been welcomed in the Stone Hall by the Chairman, Vice-Chairman and their wives.

Menu for 1927
>   **Toasts:** Hors d'Oeuvres Assortis
>   **Soup:** Clear turtle ; Ox tail
>   **Fish:** Paupiettes of Sole Alexandra
>   **Entrée:** Casserole of deche Montmorency
>   **Relèves:** Roast Haunders of Venison or Roast Saddle of Mutton
>   **Sweets:** Ice Pudding, Dane Blanche
>   Cheese Butter Biscuits
>   **Dessert:** Coffee

Toasts
1. **"The King"** Proposed by the Chairman
2. **"Our Imperial Forces"** Proposed by Mr Richard Combe JP
   To respond: Captain H.R.H. Dorman Smith.
   Songs: (a) "A Birthday" Cowan
      (b) "Songs my Mother Taught me" Dvorak
   Miss Pauline Carter
3. **"The Bishops of the Diocese and Clergy of all Denominations"**
   Proposed by Mr F.A.Morgan
   To respond: The Rector of Farnham
   Mr Middleton Woods (Humerist)
4. **"The Venison Dinner and the Town and Trade of Farnham"**
   Proposed by Mr E.J.Holland JP (Chairman Surrey County Council)
   To respond: Mr C.E.Borelli JP (Chairman Farnham U.D.C.)
   Song: "Beloved" M. Browning Fairlie (Miss Pauline Carter)
5. **"The Visitors"**. Proposed by Mr A.G.Mardon JP., CC
   To respond: The Mayor of Aldershot (Major H.Foster)
   Mr Middleton Woods. (Humerist)
6. **"The Chairman"** Proposed by Mr Scott Evans

Dress was optional, but white tie would have been expected for the top table.

The town was soon to receive another silver cup. At the 1928 Dinner Mr C.E.Borelli announced that he desired to present to the town a cup. It would be a replica of a cup held at Corpus Christi College, Oxford, reputed to have been given by Catherine of Aragon in 1515 to Bishop Joy. This would be a reminder of the Bishops of Winchester who used to be Lords of the Manor of Farnham for many years. It would also be a memento to his two years as Chairman of the U.D.C., and also mark the 100 years since the foundation of his business. This cup was used at subsequent dinners for drinking the Loyal Toast. Its present whereabouts is unknown.

In 1930 about 300 acres of Farnham Park were bought from the Ecclesiastical Commissioners by the Farnham U.D.C., for the sum of £10,175. A number of covenants were imposed. The Park must not be used for horse or dog racing; the council was to use the Park at all times as an open space within the meaning of the Open Spaces Act 1906, and the use of the recreation ground to be within the meaning of the Public Health Acts. The Park would continue to be used by the general public for cricket, football and other games, but the transfer of ownership represented another minor reduction in the influence of the Bishop in the affairs of the town, and a corresponding increase in secular control.

Unemployment remained a serious problem. Only remnants of the hop industry remained, with no evidence of anything taking its place. In 1931 concern at official level had intensified to the position where the Aldershot and District Employment Committee had written to the Council making reference to the number of unemployed in the area, and expressing the hope that the Urban District Council would not fail to press forward with any reasonable schemes of work which might help to absorb some of the local unemployed, and those being drafted into the area from Wales and the industrial midlands. The creation of programmes to provide work for large numbers of manual workers became a priority. The provision of new highways was one obvious solution. Local schemes included the widening of Waverley Lane, Crondall Lane, and improvements to Coopers Corner.

The 1931 dinner was held on the 3rd December. The guest of honour was Mr Chuter Ede, who was at that time Vice-Chairman S.C.C. Later he was to enter parliament and become a Home Secretary. He was not, he admitted, a son of Farnham, but his great grandfather had been born at Abbey Street in 1822, and had been present at the churchyard when William Cobbett was buried. He had seen Daniel O'Connell at the graveside.

The 142nd dinner in 1932 was marked by the first attendance of Bishop Greig (1927-1934) on his return to Farnham Castle as a resident. Before being taken to the dinner he was honoured by a public welcome at The Institute. Such was the enthusiasm of the townspeople at his arrival. The proceedings were unusually interrupted by the relentless demands of government, when Sir Arthur Michael Samuel, MP., left hurriedly to answer a three line whip. The toast to 'The Venison Dinner and the Town and Trade of Farnham' was proposed by Mr F.A.Morgan, the esteemed Headmaster of Farnham Grammar School. (As befits a school of renown, his respected successor, George Baxter, and subsequently, when the school became Farnham College, Kathleen Kimber, spoke at later dinners.)

A record attendance of 115 was recorded at the Bush Hotel on Wednesday, 10th November, 1934, when Mr Alan Tice presided. A leading public figure, he was a County Alderman and one of the few remaining hop growers. Apologies were received from Lord Midleton, Mr Chuter Ede and Mr Lloyd George. In proposing the toast to "The Bishop", Mr A.J.Stevens gave an interesting account of a rebellious act against the Bishop by local people over 100 years ago. It appeared that the usually popular Bishop Sumner was for some reason in bad odour. (In 1833 he had spoken against the Reform Bill). Some evilly disposed individuals prepared an elaborate effigy for November 5th. This 'Guy

Fawkes' was stored ready for the occasion in the yard of the Old Bull & Crown, in Castle Street. Mr Stevens's great, great, grandfather heard about it, entered the yard, found the effigy and buried it in the garden of 62, Castle Street.

The Chairman took the opportunity to inform the assembly that Sir John Jarvis, High Sheriff for Surrey, would be attending the next meeting of the Council to explain the Surrey Scheme to help Jarrow. Widespread poverty, due to the lack of employment in this Durham town, had struck a cord in the national conscience. Surrey had responded with Sir John touring the county to suggest fund raising schemes. By the 16th November, 1934, the Surrey Fund for the Relief of Durham had reached £22,277.18s 6d. Farnham played its part with generous donations from churches, schools and other organisations. Sir John visited Jarrow, and reported that Surrey had provided paint, distemper and wall paper for tenants. He later received a Royal Commendation for his untiring effort.

It was an unusual occurrence for a guest to leave the dinner before the final toast, still even more unusual for someone to be required to leave. A unique occasion arose in 1935, when it was decided to engage an entertainer 'in a lighter vein', together with a singer. The entertainer came on after the first speech, and for ten minutes told a string of naughty stories. This was a calamity. No-one applauded. There were looks of disgust. The Chairman told the Deputy Clerk to pay him off, and make sure he caught the next train back to London. The singer gave an extra turn, to warm applause, and, no doubt, general relief.

The dinners had always provided opportunities for speakers to promote ideas for the betterment of the town. The 146th dinner heard Lord Baden Powell (son of the founder of the Scouts movement) appeal for a museum for Farnham. Farnham was a treasurehouse of antiquarian interest, right through the ages, and we didn't know half enough of its history, because its hidden in the ground. He pleaded for Farnham to establish its own museum. He had heard of a working man in Farnham, who said he was willing to give up smoking, in order to put just 2s 6d weekly into a fund to provide a museum. (Farnham did get its museum, but not until 1961) He then referred to the electrification of the railway, and suggested - perhaps the company will get electrified one of these days, and we shall have a new station. At any rate I hope they will give it a lick of paint before the coronation.

The dinners continued uninterrupted, with Wednesday now being the preferred day. The toasts, containing references to the town's lack of a charter, and the proposed relief road for through traffic, were interspersed with songs and musical items; toasts to 'The Chairman' invariably being drunk with musical honours, and the evenings concluding with Auld Lang Syne, and the national anthem. As usual, the venison being donated by Lord Midleton.

In 1937, the 147th, the guest of honour, Sir Philip Henriques, Chairman S.C.C. spoke of the coming by-pass. He felt that the townspeople of Farnham would eventually come to the conclusion that the right action had been taken, because the Park would have been preserved intact, and they would have a fine by-pass to the south to prevent people being killed more than necessary. At the time, an alternative scheme had been proposed for a new road through the park, but it was not supported at government level.

The following advertisement appeared in the Farnham Herald in advance of the 1938 dinner: "Applications for tickets for the Venison Dinner to be held on the 29th November, 1938 to be made to the Deputy Clerk without delay. Accommodation limited". (After the war an announcement was routinely placed in the local press to invite members of the public to apply for tickets.) This was the last dinner to be held before the outbreak of the second World War, and the last to be held at the Bush Hotel. Mrs Stroud MP., Chairman of the Council presided. The Provost (The Very Rev. E.G. Southern) made a plea for financial support for the new cathedral at Guildford. He would be holding a series of Cathedral weeks when he would be asking the diocese to donate a total of £80,000 to ensure the completion of the first part of the cathedral. They had just signed a contract with the builders for completion in 1941, when payment would be due. He remarked that Farnham was not the centre of the new diocese; Guildford was. If Farnham had made representations when the new boundaries were being drawn, changes may have been possible and the Parish Church would have become the Cathedral with the Bishop living there. The Lord Bishop of Guildford (John. V. Macmillan, 1934 -1949) was represented by his son. One guest -Lady Snowden, (widow of the former Chancellor of the Exchequer) had to leave early - Il.00pm! - due to another engagement and long before the flood of oratory had concluded.

Mrs Stroud said that she was exceedingly proud to become the first woman Chairman of the U.D.C., and the first to preside at the Venison Dinner. In referring to the relief road now being provided to the South of Farnham, she said it was needed to alleviate the congestion in the main streets. Mr Hamilton Jones, Chairman of the Chamber of Commerce, spoke of the role of the Chamber. It's primary object was to promote trade in the town. People had to be encouraged to enter the town. To this end a one-way traffic scheme was needed. (Sixty years later, the traffic problems are no nearer to solution.)

During the war years the dinners were suspended.

The revival of the Dinner in 1949 was a spectacular event. It was the first to be held at Farnham Castle, though it was not to return for another thirteen years. By special arrangement with the Southern Electricity Board the exterior of the Castle was floodlit for the evening, thereby providing a magnificent spectacle of orange and green lighting effects, which could be viewed to the full from the surrounding hills. The principal guest was the Bishop-Elect of Guildford, the Rt. Rev. H.C. Montgomery-Campbell (1949-1956). Mr W.H. Emery, Chairman of the U.D.C. presided. Further evidence of the recognition of the changes in relationship within the town was given when the Bishop-Elect commented on changes that had occurred since the 17th century. As a townsman of Farnham he would humbly submit himself to the

Chairman of the Council and others in authority. In the old days the Burgesses and Bailiffs of the town owed humble allegiance to the Bishop, from whose hand the town held its charter as a Borough. He explained that it was indeed a privilege and a joy to come to Farnham. He had many childhood memories of Farnham as his great-uncle and aunt lived at Crondall.

There was a tendency for compliments to flow freely during the speeches. One which was particularly acceptable was given by Sir Harry Brittain in reply to a toast. He had always been given to understand that one of the outstanding features of Farnham was the beauty of the Farnham ladies, and since becoming a neighbour he had proved the truth of that. The Farnham mother with two marriageable daughters would never have to intone the lament, which he once heard elsewhere:

> I have two girls, a couple of pearls,
> What mother could wish for more?
> But I see no sign of a couple of swine,
> To cast those pearls before.

Among the numerous acknowledgements for assistance was one to Mr C.E. Borelli for the loan of silver and the gift of grapes. (Known as the 'Borelli Grapes', they were provided annually at the October council meeting by Mr Borelli from his own vine.) Throughout the evening entertainment had been provided by musicians in the Minstrels Gallery, and by artistes providing songs, mainly scottish, between the speeches.

In 1949 Francis Morgan was moved to portray the views of the chief victim - the buck!

> Was it to feed the vanity of men,
> Defiant of the Damoclean axe,
> Was it for this, I left my Highland glen,
> Butchered to fill the maws of Sassenachs?
> Arise, Sir Stafford, smite them with thy wrath,
> And next year make them feast on rabbit broth

In 1950, reported as being 'A sign of the times', the arrangements for the dinner were cancelled. It was to have been held at the Castle on the 22nd November. Some 200 invitations had been sent out as usual, but as only 47 acceptances had been received, there was clearly a lack of support. It was deemed that at least 100 guests were needed to make ends meet. The ticket price of 25/- each was only just sufficient to cover expenses on a carefully prepared budget. It was not to have been in any way an extravagant meal. On the other hand it was felt that it was owed to tradition not to lower the standard, bearing in mind the many distinguished persons who, by custom, were invited to the feast as guests of Farnham. The previous year over 120 had attended.

The lack of interest did not extend into 1951. The 151st was held at the Memorial Hall on Friday, 7th December, with nearly 150 guests. The arrangements had been made by a town committee, which may account for the significant change in the programme to provide dancing after the meal to the music of Jimmy Ross and his orchestra. The event was significant in other ways. On display were the famous Byworth Cup and the grant of Arms by the College of Heralds.

Entertainment was provided by the Farnham Junior Children's Choir, conducted by Mrs Mary Joynes. The choir was to become known as Farnham's ambassadors of song, and was to win both national and international acclaim. As the girls grew older the choir became the Farnham Singers, before bowing out in 1987.

In 1953, the dinner, again at the Memorial Hall, was graced by the presence of Dr Cyril Garbett, Archbishop of York. Dr Garbett had many fond memories of Farnham, as he had been born at Tongham Vicarage, and used to ride a pony when travelling to Farnham Grammar School. While driving to Farnham for the dinner, he felt that he was coming home.

His Honour Judge Gordon Clark enlivened the 156th dinner with a legal view of the origin of the Venison Feast. He had indulged in a great deal of research to discover the history, when he learned that he was going to speak. He asserted that the history of the dinner boiled down to what was known in the East End and Soho as 'protection'. What happened in the middle ages was that the people of Farnham came to the Castle, and suggested to the Bishop that the deer should be protected from the poachers from Elstead and Seale, and from over the boarder at Aldershot. Naturally, the gamekeepers needed a little reward. The Bishop took the hint, and instructed that a haunch should be provided. That, in simple terms, is the history of the dinner.

In praising the quality of the venison, he recalled the lines of Oliver Goldsmith; "Thank my Lord for the venison, for fairer and fatter n'er ranged in a forest, nor smoked on a platter".

But the expanding political influence over the dinner was not to be checked. The toast to 'The Venison Dinner and the Trade and Town of Farnham', had been modified to 'The Venison Dinner and the Town of Farnham'. The preponderance of council Chairmen and Mayors ensured that the major content of the speeches revolved around local authority affairs during the current year. Those indifferent to local policies and controversies would have found the speeches profoundly boring, as all of the points laboured, however skilfully, would have been aired fully in the local press. This was well illustrated in 1954 when three matters, albeit of some importance, received prolonged attention. The first was that preliminary work in connection with a petition for the restoration of the towns charter was nearing completion. The second was that the Waverley Abbey ruins were to be preserved with generous help from County Hall, and many charitable friends from Farnham and the surrounding area. Thirdly, that the Surrey County Council had agreed with the Ministry of Transport to allow the County to complete the first part of the by-pass works as a very high priority indeed. 'Trade' would no longer receive a high priority, with words of praise being restricted to fellow politicians.

Undoubtedly, the highlight of the 1950's dinners was in 1959, when the principal guest of honour at the Bush Hotel was Field Marshall Viscount Montgomery. The capacity crowd of 116, and the substantial waiting list, testified to the popularity of the dinner that year. In proposing the toast to "The Venison Dinner and the Town of Farnham, 'Monty' began in a light vein. Although not a resident of Farnham - he resided at Isington Mill, Bentley - he did come to Farnham to collect his old-age pension. He recalled the first day he entered Farnham Post Office. The lady behind the counter said to him, 'Do you really need this?' He replied "I most certainly do. After all, one must live". On a more serious note, he recounted his two day meeting earlier that year with Mr Kruschev, who had probably got, in his two hands, more power than had ever been given to anybody on this earth; it was his (Monty's) view that he genuinely wished to sort this thing out peacefully.

(The 'Cold War' situation had not yet been resolved). "If there was one thing the Russian leaders did not want it was war". He told Kruschev that he was not a politician, just a simple soldier who spoke the truth. That seemed to surprise Kuschev. 'Monty' had last visited Moscow in 1947 to stay with Stalin who was a friend. "He (Monty) had many odd friends, but he wouldn't go into the jungle with some of them!" He concluded by referring to his frequent visits to the town - "I would like to say this. When I come to Farnham for that (pension) purpose, or for other matters, I do not think I have been in a town or city where one is received in the shops and post office, and everywhere else with such extraordinary kindness and courtesy. It is very striking, and I want to pay tribute to it".

The sudden death in 1960 of the Bishop of Guildford, Dr Ivor Watkins, led to the postponement of the dinner until the following April. One of the principal guests would have been the Surrey and England cricket captain, P.B.H.May, who lived at Cranleigh. Regrettably he was not available on the revised date. The newly elected Bishop, The Rt. Rev. G.E.Reindorp also declined to attend as he was not accepting public engagements until after he had been enthroned.

He did attend, with his wife, the second dinner that year in November. For the first time for many years, the Bishop was invited to assist with cutting the first slice of venison. The Bishop spoke about the new cathedral. In countering criticism in the press, that the cathedral was badly sited and not popular, he stated that on Tuesday last, one thousand people gathered there to hear an hour long lecture; up to Tuesday night 999 conducted parties had been taken round. Probably 3 million people had visited it, and 110,000 had worshipped there. This was the cathedral to which it was said - "No-one would go because it was in the wrong place".

The future of the Castle had at last been secured. It had not been occupied by the Bishop since 1956 and was in a state of acute disrepair.The Church Commissioners had stated that a diocesan use was difficult, if not impossible to find, but had now agreed a lease with Oversea Service for a period of 60 years. Oversea Service was a non-

At the 1963 Dinner, white ties remained the expected dress at the top table.

profit making organisation, which existed, in particular, to provide courses for people about to visit, or take up residence overseas. The courses were designed to increase their knowledge of the countries and peoples, and to fit them as representatives of Western Christian civilisation.

Throughout the 1960's and early 1970's, the dinners continued to be held at the Castle. The format had settled down to become what was virtually an annual civic dinner, attended by civic dignatories from the County Council and surrounding local authorities, with seven speeches, and entertainment ranging from a military string band, to vocal renderings from the Farnham Amateur Operatic Society. The Bishop of Guildford remained the principal guest, with the Bishop of Dorking deputising for him on occasion.

National events were not overlooked. In 1966 guests observed a silence in respect of the appalling disaster at Aberfan, when so many school children died as a result of a pit spoilage heap sliding and demolishing a school. A deep sadness swept throughout the nation.

On a brighter note, the choice of the principal guest was sometimes not unconnected with the pursuit of a purely local authority advantage. 1967 saw the launch of the new (Redgrave) theatre project. It was considered prudent to obtain the goodwill of the Arts Council of Great Britain. It was no coincidence that Lord Goodman, their President, was invited as their principal guest that year. He rose to the occasion by commenting on the invitations he received, when he said, "I'm rarely asked for my blue eyes".

Of technical significance was the installation of a public address system in 1970 for the first time. It was reported subsequently that this innovation 'made no small contribution to the success of the evening'

In 1972, a third cup having local connections was to make its appearance at the dinner. The Council had acquired the William Cobbett Silver Cup, and had requested that it be put on display and used for the Loyal Toast.

During the 1970's proposals for the further re-organisation of local government had been gaining momentum. There had been a boundary Commission in 1945, followed by the Report of the Radcliffe-Maude Commission in 1969. Larger units of administration were recommended. The 1972 Local Government Act received Royal Assent on October 26th, 1972. Authorities were encouraged to amalgamate with their neighbours. Locally, Farnham U.D.C. was to be combined with Godalming Borough Council, Haslemere U.D.C., and Hambledon R.D.C. to form Waverley District Council, with new offices to be built at Godalming.

The last Venison Dinner to be held under the benevolence of the U.D.C. was held at the Castle on the 2nd November, 1973. The organising committee comprised:

    Cllr A.G.Hurdle. (Chairman Farnham U.D.C.)
    Cllr K.J.Chandler. (Vice-Chairman Farnham U.D.C.)
    Mr D. Coyne. (President, Farnham Chamber of Commerce)
    Mr K.Kime. (President, Rotary Club of Farnham)
    Mr H.H.Lancaster. (Deputy Clerk, Farnham U.D.C.)

The Great Hall was resplendent with the top table having red leather chairs from the Council Chamber; the remainder being obtained from the Memorial Hall. Floral arrangements were from the West Street nursery.

The public address system continued to be generously donated by Mr K.J.Chandler.

Catering was by E.H.Clark (Caterers) Ltd who also provided the candelabra and linen napkins.

The cost of tickets remained at £3.50, the same as the previous year, which probably accounted for the financial imbalance of £120. It appeared that while 109 tickets were sold, the attendance was about 150.

The menu was somewhat modest in view of the significance of the occasion.

    Pâté maison

    Creme of asparagus soup or Consommé au pot

    Roast haunch of venison, Chateau potatoes, Duchess potatoes,
      Brussels sprouts, Garden peas

    Soufflé glacé praline

    Cheese & biscuits. Celery.

    Coffee

Background piano from the Minstrels Gallery by Mrs W.O. Manning. As expected the speakers made references to the imminent, but to some,fateful, re-organisation.

The Chairman of the committee, Mr Hurdle, voiced concern over the future of the Venison Dinner. Summing up the position, he stated: "It's not a civic dinner, its roots go deeper. It was a dinner of the town of Farnham." The organising committee had now to consider the position that would emerge in 1974, when the re-organisation of local government would have been accomplished, and the Farnham U.D.C. would no longer exist. It was important that the town's sole remaining traditional function should not be allowed to lapse. It fell to the few who had worked so hard over the past years to maintain continuity, and to that end, to continue to work together into the future, albeit in a different independent capacity.

On the 31st March, 1974 the Farnham U.D.C. became defunct.

Farnham Consultative Committee
1974 - 1984

On the first April 1974 Farnham became incorporated in the administrative area of the new Waverley District (subsequently Borough) Council, with all property, powers and duties transferred to Waverley as the successor authority.

Several of the U.D.C. councillors, who had assisted with the organisation of the Venison Dinner, stood for election to the new authority. The following were successful: Messrs Chandler, Cordier, Hurdle and Lawrence.

Although it had always been recognised that the Venison Dinner was not, historically, a civic responsibility, there was a possibility that Waverley, as the successor authority, and whose Mayor was Farnham's first citizen, might wish to encourage the continuation of the dinner, and be prepared to have a degree of involvement.

While the matter was being aired between the former U.D.C. councillors, Waverley, pre-occupied with the more important problems of re-organisation, determined that with Farnham being the largest centre of population in their district there was a need to obtain the views of the town on matters of a purely local nature; in particular, to obtain their views on planning applications.

Accordingly the Farnham Consultative Committee, consisting of the 19 Farnham members, was soon established. Meetings were held in the Council Chamber, South Street. At their first meeting on Ist May, 1974, a sub-committee comprising Messrs Aylett, Cordier, Chandler, and Hurdle was set up to consider, in conjunction with representatives of Farnham Castle, the Chamber of Commerce, the Rotary Club of Farnham and the Farnham Society, the possibility of arranging a Venison Dinner during 1974. All of them had previous experience of organising the dinner.

The sub-committee accepted that the benevolence previously shown by the U.D.C. no longer existed, and that unless continued by Waverley the dinner would have to be financially self-supporting, with the administration carried out by their own members. Members would have to purchase their own tickets and foot any loss, in the event of one being incurred.

Mr Hurdle, Chairman of the sub-committee wrote to Waverley, stating that the responsibility for arranging the Venison Dinner had for many years been accepted by the Chairman of the U.D.C., with the deficit being met out of his allowances; the only direct contribution made, since the Castle became the venue, being the free use of transport to provide and remove chairs and tables, the setting up, the supply of floral decorations and the provision of a car parking attendant. Would Waverley be prepared to do the same?

The request was considered by Waverley's Leisure Committee who declined the offer. The full council later approved the minute without comment, but Waverley did on occasion provide transport on a rechargeable basis.

The 1974 dinner went ahead with the following committee:
- A.G.Hurdle (Chairman)
- R.F.Cordier
- K.J.Chandler,
- W.E.Grenville-Grey (Administrator, Farnham Castle)
- H.H.Lancaster
- P.A.F.Aylett
- A.L.Addy (President, Rotary Club of Farnham)
- A.Windsor (President, Farnham Society)
- Mrs R.Rathmell (Hon. Secretary)

It was agreed that it was of vital importance that the standards of past years should be maintained, with the chief guest being the Lord Bishop. Also that tickets should be made freely available to members of the public, with no reservations before the publicly advertised date of availability, which would be early September. In the past very few tickets had been available to the general public, as the twenty one councillors, the Chief Officers, their wives, husbands and friends, together with other civic leaders, and the speakers, had taken the majority.

The dinner had now reverted to the status it held in the late eighteenth, nineteenth and early twentieth centuries. i.e. organised by an independent committee comprising representatives of trade and commerce within the town on a self-financing basis, while remaining strictly apolitical.

The dinner was held at the Castle on the 8th November. Toasts were limited to two with the Lord Bishop of Guildford, the Rt. Rev. David Brown (1973-1982) giving the principal speech. The Lord Bishop of Dorking, the Rt. Rev. K.D.Evans, was also present. Another notable guest was the Rt. Hon. Maurice MacMillan M.P. In view of the reduction in the number of speeches, it was agreed that musical entertainment should be provided. Local entertainers, the Hilary Folk, were engaged, with Mr V. Scribbans acting as toastmaster.

The event was warmly received, with 138 tickets being sold at £3.75 each. The five course meal was provided by Clark's of Farnborough, soon to become the regular caterer. With the reduction of deer herds in the South, the venison to-day is obtained from a supplier in Scotland.

Without the administrative and other support, the dinner resulted in a small financial loss. This was made good by Mrs Anne Hoath, a member of the Consultative Committee, as it appeared that the committee had achieved the correct formula; had secured the future of the dinner, and would be able to continue on a self-financing basis. This prognosis proved to be correct.

At that time sponsorship was not considered, but a benefactor was soon to appear.

Standards of dress continued to change in subtle ways. For many years white tie had been the expected dress at the top table. With the desire for less formality, and the growing preference for the more convenient dinner jacket, the event would now be black tie.

Of more importance was the need to contain the length of the speeches, and to ensure that the evening concluded well before 11.30pm.

Following the Loyal Toast, the speeches would in future be restricted to the two time-honoured toasts, with responses, which formed the historical foundation of the dinner, and expressed the strong bond between the town and the Lord Bishops, namely: "The Bishop of the Diocese and the Clergy of all Denominations" and "The Venison Dinner and the Town of Farnham".

Regrettably, in 1975 the Castle became unavailable. The only other location obtainable at short notice was the Memorial Hall. The position was unchanged in 1976, when it was held for the first time at the Maltings. On this occasion the catering was done by Finbows of Cambridge Place. Neither the Memorial Hall or the Maltings possessed the ambience deemed appropriate for holding the Venison Dinner, although both venues were well supported and warmly received. The booking for 1977 at the Castle was revoked, as it conflicted with bookings to celebrate the tercentenary of the restoration of the Great Hall, during the episcopacy of Bishop Morley. It was probably due to the apprehension felt by the public about returning to the Maltings, that the 1977 dinner had to be cancelled through lack of support.

1979 saw a welcome return to the Great Hall at the Castle after several years absence. Catering was again by Finbows, who served the 175 guests with a trout apiece, 60lbs of Devon venison, 48 dozen profiteroles with 2½ gallons of cream. Tickets were sold at £6.45 each. The colourful tables which were laid with crimson tablecloths and red candles would have presented a striking scene when viewed from the galleries.

The date of the dinner was now stabilised. It would be held on the second or third Friday in November.

The 1980 dinner was one of convivial euphoria. Advertised as the 178th, it was in fact the 179th. This was only one of many occasions throughout the decades when miscounting occurred! In the absence of Arthur Hurdle, the Chairman, Lady Anson presided, and cut the first slice. She was only the second woman to carry out these duties. The first was Mrs Stroud in 1938. The evening was enlivened by the spontaneous rendering of "Happy birthday" to the Bishop, when it was announced that it was his birthday. The dinners continued with noticeably less civic pomposity. It was now inappropriate for speakers to recite the lengthy aspirations of the local authority, which many considered boring. The new Bishop of Guildford, Michael Adie (1983-1994) speaking at the 1983 dinner said that he was still suffering from the cultural shock of coming from rural Lincolnshire, to the wealthy county of Surrey. Once a curate in Sunderland, he hadn't quite realised that in the south of England people looked at things differently. He quoted the story of a local 6 year old boy, whose younger sister had lost her first tooth. The boy knew about the tooth fairy, and decided to carry out the transformation himself. Instead of putting 5p under his sister's pillow, he put his father's credit card!

The dinners continued at the Castle without interruption until the Consultative Committee was abolished in 1984. This decision meant that the Council Chamber was no longer available to the Venison Dinner Committee. with the result that from then on, meetings were held at the home of Donald Scott, one of the members.

Farnham Town Council 1984 -

Farnham Parish Council was established on the Ist April, 1984. At their first meeting on the 6th April they resolved to adopt the style of Town Council, with a Town Mayor instead of a Chairman. It was axiomatic that their first Town Mayor, Brig. Alan Smallman should speak at the 182nd Venison Dinner held on the 16th November that year. In responding to the toast "The Venison Dinner and the Town of Farnham", he praised the former Farnham Consultative Committee who were people of energy, dedication and concern. They had kept alive the Farnham activities such as the Venison Dinner. He saw the Town Council as being a legally constituted separate body. There was no hierarchical command spreading downward from the County Council, through Waverley to the Town Council. The town was prospering well, but suffering from indigestion and circulatory problems." (A statement that would be echoed today.)

In 1985 a Working Party was set up to consider 'Civic functions and links with the town'. The Working Party reported that they would like the Venison Dinner to become the Farnham Town Council's Annual Civic Dinner, as in the past, and re-establish the Council's link with this historic event. At the same time they re-affirmed the principal of minimal spending of the rate on functions. It was hoped that the existing Venison Dinner Committee would continue to run it on behalf of, or in the name of, Farnham Town Council.

At that time, three of the Venison Dinner Committee - Mr Cordier, (Chairman), Mrs Hoath and Mr Lawrence, were also elected members of Farnham Town Council, but they were not members of the Working Party.

The Town Council's Committee declared that in future the Town Mayor and Husband/Wife, would join the Chairman and his wife, to receive guests in The Minstrels Gallery. Also that the Town Mayor would cut the first slice of venison instead of the Chairman, and that The Town Mayor and Town Clerk would become ex officio members of the Venison Dinner Committee. There was no prior negotiation with the Venison Dinner Committee who accepted the imposed (unenforceable) conditions without comment.

In 1986 the sole remaining link between Farnham and the Bishop of Winchester was severed irrevocably. The Lordship of the Manor of Farnham which had remained dormant since it reverted to the Ecclesiastical Commissioners on becoming vacant in 1869, following the death of Bishop Sumner, was sold to a resident of Farnham. Any sale of a Manor would have to follow certain criteria as the policy of the Commissioners was a passive one. Sales would be considered only in areas where the Lordship did not own a significant amount of land, or possess substantial mineral interests. Most importantly, the area was not within a cathedral city. In addition the purchaser would have to meet numerous conditions. The purchaser subsequently sold in 1987 when the Lordship was put up for auction. In 1988 the Lordship was purchased by

Ken Kent of Farnham.

Traffic problems were never far from the thoughts of the speakers at the dinner. It came as no surprise when, in 1989, John Wainwright, who had retired after 20 years as the local planning chief, said - "There was no real answer to Farnham's traffic problems. - The same conclusion that had been arrived at by the architects of the 1947 Farnham Town Plan". They believed the by-pass should have gone north of the town. It hadn't and therefore a two level junction at Hickley's corner was their solution. Not content with that, they also proposed two new roads over the by-pass and the railway.

After a lapse of 27 years the revered name of Viscount Montgomery of Alemain appeared again on the menu. On this occasion, the 184th dinner, it was the son of 'Monty', who was at that time a director of the Castle. The dinners continued to be successful social events, well supported by the people of the town. A european dimension was introduced in 1988 when Dr Klinkhammer, the Burgermeister of Mayen-Koblenz attended. Waverley had twinned with Mayen-Koblenz in 1977. This was the first occasion that a representative from that town had attended, and was to be the forerunner of a series of visits from civic dignatories from Adernach, with whom Farnham twinned in 1992.

In 1990 the Chairman of the Venison Dinner Committee, Frank Cordier, (elected annually by the committee) was also Town Mayor and played the dual role, as there was no Vice-Chairman. A warm welcome

1990 Dinner:
The 'first slice' is cut by Frank Cordier in his dual role as Chairman and Town Mayor.

was given to Dr G. Kuffmann, the Oberburgermeister of Andernach making his first appearance at the dinner. Preliminary discussions regarding a possible twinning were in progress. The dinner provided an opportunity for him to meet townspeople, and experience Farnham's remaining traditional event.

There appeared to be no call for change in the proceedings at the dinner, as there was no difficulty in selling tickets, and no complaints about the length or content of the speeches. Speakers had been chosen carefully, given time limits, and advice on the content expected.

The next Town Mayor, Lt Col. M. Bransby-Williams, considered that the historic Venison Dinner should be run by the Town Council and not by an independent committee, and brought the matter before his fellow councillors. He was highly critical of the committee. He viewed the dinner as having been run as a private party, with the committee deciding who should be the speakers, and who should have tickets. He had almost had to beg for tickets. "The venison Dinner was essentially for giving speeches, but for some years no topic of great importance to Farnham has actually been raised." He would very much like to have had a say in the choice of those speakers, and he thought the Town Mayor should unquestionably preside, and should take the opportunity to "report to the people of Farnham". He requested permanent co-option of one town councillor on the committee and some priority in the allocation of tickets. This should be "with a view to the complete takeover of the Venison Dinner on the Ist December, 1991."

There followed suggestions that there should be open discussions with the Venison Dinner Committee to consider the takeover. The Town Mayor's proposal was seconded, and lost by four votes to six.

The Venison Dinner Committee duly met and considered the "take over" proposal which they rejected. During the ten years of the Farnham Consultative Committee they had organised the dinners successfully, and had maintained the tradition. The dinners had been well supported by the community who were obviously not desirous of any change. In any case, the Farnham Town Council already had ample opportunity at their Annual Town Meeting to explain their activities to the inhabitants of the town. This meeting was required by law.

They did confirm that they would continue to honour their commitment to the Town Mayor joining the reception line, cutting the first slice of venison, joining the other guests for drinks and sitting on the committee for the year of office. Except for the Town Mayor there would be no other priority in the allocation of tickets, as in the past only about 20 had been available for members of the general public. Tickets would continue to be sold on a "first come, first served" basis. None would be reserved in advance.

The Town Mayor decided not to attend the dinner, which had a capacity attendance. Speakers gave the current organising committee their support; the guests responded by giving resounding applause, with thunderous table thumping. Peter White, Chairman of the Farnham

In 1992 the Town Mayor, Zora Bransby-Williams cuts the first slice. Also pictured are Ray Tindle, later to become the first President of the Committee: the Bishop of Dorking the Rt. Rev. David Wilcox, the toastmaster Peter Walters and the chef.

bench, gave his view "Keep it up, keep it as it is, the same format, we love it!" Other speakers, Norman Taylor, Director W.S.C.A.D., (now Surrey Institute of Art and Design, University College), and Gary Meyjes, past president, Farnham Chamber of Commerce echoed his sentiments.

That the dinner was held at the Castle, was due to a favourable decision by the Director, that the booking by the Venison Dinner Committee did not contravene any restrictions placed upon lettings. This decision followed a move to have the hiring of the Castle denied to the Committee. Once again, the future control of the dinner was placed in jeopardy. If the Committee's application had been rescinded, the Town Council would, presumably, have seized the opportunity to take over the booking, and, as a consequence, the dinner.

The 190th dinner held on the 13th November, 1992 was marked by references to momentous changes in the structure of the church. The Bishop of Dorking, the Rt. Rev. David Wilcox, commenting on the recent decision to allow women to be ordained, had "no doubt that it was the right thing to do". The Rector of Farnham, the Rev. Andrew Tuck, said that the event "would bring tremendous enrichment to the church". "We're not throwing away our traditions, we're discovering new gifts". He paid tribute to the Bishop of Guildford, the Rt. Rev. Michael Adie, who first moved the motion in favour of the ordination of women, and spoke in favour of it. Another speaker, Denis Stone, Vice-Chairman, Farnham Castle Newspapers, whose grandmother was born in Farnham in 1849, singled out three people who he said had given so much to the town during his lifetime - Charles Borelli, for striving to preserve the Georgian and Victorian buildings in the town, Canon Hedley Wilds for restoring the parish church in the 1950's, and Peter Drakes-Wilkes for developing the Farnham Maltings. On a sporting note, he continued - one year Rowledge must win the UK Village Cup competition! "They have been so close on several occasions."

The Byworth Cup was again used for the Loyal Toast. It was 'on loan' from Waverley as a gesture of goodwill.

Town Clerk, Fred Culver takes the Byworth Cup to the Dinner in 1994.

At the next meeting of the Venison Dinner Committee it was reported that numerous letters of congratulation had been received.

The controversy over the control of the dinner appeared to have subsided, yet without further consultation, the Town Council resolved formally at their Council Meeting held on the 9th January, 1992 as follows:

(a) That the Venison Dinner be re-affirmed as a civic event with the annual organisation being carried out on behalf of the Town Council by the existing Venison Dinner Committee which originated in 1974. (This refers to the independent Committee formed following the demise of the U.D.C.)

(b) That the civic connection continue as follows:

1) The Town Mayor to continue as a member of the Venison Dinner Committee with the Town Clerk being appointed as an additional member.

2) The Town Mayor (and Mayoress) together with the Chairman of the Venison Dinner Committee, to receive the guests at the start of the function.

3) The Town Mayor to cut the first slice of venison.

4) The Town Mayor to propose the loyal toast.

There the matter appears to rest. The dinners continue to be held at the Castle, with the principal toast alternating between the Bishop of Guildford, and the Suffragen Bishop of Dorking. (Dorking was in the Winchester Diocese until 1927. The See was in abeyance from 1909 - 1968. There have been three Suffragen Bishops: Kenneth D. Evans, David P. Wilcox and Ian J. Brackley)

In step with inflation, the cost of a ticket had risen from £18. 50 in 1990 to £23 in 1993.

1998 Dinner. The speakers were, Joseph Sheldon, Chairman of Abbeyfield, the Rt. Rev. John Gladwyn, Bishop of Guildford, Peter De Voile, Headmaster, Frensham Heights and Pamela Woodroffe, Chairman, Farnham Maltings Association.

The Byworth Cup came into prominence during 1994, when a request from the Farnham Joint Consultative Committee for the Cup to be transferred from Waverley to the Farnham Town Council was considered.

While Waverley was legally the owner of the Cup, it was felt that the benefactor gave the Cup to the people of Farnham with the intention that they should enjoy it. Accordingly, it was agreed that it should be transferred on permanent loan to the Town Council. It is now on display annually at the Venison Dinner and used by the Town Mayor to drink the Loyal Toast.

The civic twinning with Andernach has been supported and strengthened by the formation of the Farnham/Andernach Friendship Association. Numerous personal friendships have been formed, and frequent reciprocal visits arranged. The Association has hosted several visits by civic leaders from Andernach, members of their Andernach/Farnham Friendship Association, and language students. This relationship, with the offer of accommodation, has been of immense value when inviting our German twins to the Dinner.

In 1994 Herr A. Hütton, the Oberburgermeister of Andernach, with Herr and Frau M. Fuchs attended, while in 1996 a larger group comprising the Chairman and members of the Andernach/Farnham Friendship Association and their interpreter Herr G. von Blohn, led by their Burgermeister, Herr F. Breil, made the Venison Dinner the highlight of a prolonged visit.

The same year, Sir Ray Tindle, proprietor of the Farnham Herald, graciously accepted an invitation from the Venison Dinner Committee to become their first President. With the continued support of the townspeople, the future of the Venison Dinner was now in no doubt. Yet there was one, apparently innocuous, enquiry that had been received over recent years - requests for a vegetarian meal! If this trend escalates, the committee may have to think the unthinkable - a Venison Dinner - without venison! One can foresee the spirit of Bishop Brownlow North returning to pace the upper galleries surrounding the Great Hall, arms upraised in utter horror and disbelief.

Epilogue

The Venison Dinner has, over the centuries provided snapshots of the social, religious, trade and political circumstances prevailing in Farnham during times of dynamic change. The event has provided a continuous thread running through four centuries of the town's history, and brought together all the functions and activities that blend together to form our rich heritage.

Numerous changes, some subtle, others more forceful have occurred, or been inflicted, and have always been reflected in the structure and content of the toasts.

So much for the past, and present. What of the future? Farnham is no longer a 'one product' town. The small bustling shops have remained in abundance; many of them enhancing the numerous attractive courtyards and alleys. Apart from electrical goods, two supermarkets and Woolworths, the large multiples have stayed away. Trading estates have provided local opportunities for skilled workers, particularly in the electronics industry. There is a moderate amount of commuting to London and there is a burgeoning tourist trade. Our magnificent Georgian houses still have universal appeal.

The Venison Dinner, Farnham's only remaining traditional link with its past, continues with the selfless support of the Bishops, and the continued support of the people of the town.

Those attending the dinner, as we enter the millennium, will not be maltsters, brewers, clothiers or hatters. More likely they will be professionals, financiers, proprietors of small specialist businesses, or retired. May this ancient tradition continue.

Bishop Brownlow North LL.D.
(1781 - 1820)

Bishop Brownlow North was a great friend of the first Earl of Carnarvon which may explain why this portrait hangs at Highclere Castle, near Newbury, instead of Farnham Castle.

The painting by Henry Howard was exhibited at the Royal Academy in 1818, and possibly in 1798.

There is a copy of a different portrait at Farnham Castle.

Renowned for his nepotism, the appointment of his son as Master of St Cross, Winchester, was to result in a scandal that was to fester for many years after the Bishop's death. Indeed, his own promotion to the See of Winchester was undoubtedly assisted by his elder brother's position as Prime Minister, which carried the duty to make recommendations to the Monarch.

In addition to his extensive social and charitable activities at home, he was noted for his extensive absences abroad. Both he and Mrs North were gifted botanists. They raised many rare species brought back from warmer climes, and re-planned the castle gardens.

It is stated in "A Short History and Guide to Farnham Castle" that the cedar trees in the castle grounds resulted from seeds brought back from the Lebanon by Mrs North. It is more likely that seedlings were brought from Highclere Castle, where many fine specimens survive today.It is known that seeds brought from the Lebanon were planted at Highclere in the late 18th century by plant seed collector, Bishop Stephen Pococke.

Confirmation that Highclere was the source of the Farnham cedars appears in 'The Herberts of Highclere', published by the 4th Earl of Carnarvon in 1908. He describes how he heard "that Lord North, Bishop of Winchester, carried away in a post-chaise some of the young cedars from Highclere, and that those which now thrive at Farnham are some of these. The driver of the chaise on the box was, I have been told, almost hidden by plants."

Bishop Brownlow North's coat of arms has a lion passant (gold), three fleurs de lis (silver) one crescent (dexter. silver) on a field of blue.

The Close Seasons

Prior to the twentieth century there was no statutory close-time for fox hunting and rabbit shooting, nor was there, apart from Ireland, a close-time for deer or hares. There was an 'Unwritten law' which the sportsman respected, under which the hunting or stalking of deer was restricted to 12th August to the 12th October for stags, and from 10th November to the 10th of March for hinds. During the latter part of this century, a number of statutes have been enacted, and subsequently modified. The killing of deer is presently controlled by the provisions of the Deer Act 1991.

Poaching remains an offence: "If any person enters any land without consent of the owner or occupier or other lawful authority in search or pursuit of any deer with the intention of killing or injuring it he shall be guilty of an offence. Exemptions are given to the taking or killing of deer during the close season: Exemption where by way of business, a person keeps deer on land enclosed by a deer proof barrier for production of meat or other foodstuffs or skins or other by-products, or as breeding stock, and, deer conspicuously marked so as to identify them as deer kept by that person. Prohibited weapons are: Traps, snares or poisoned and stupifying bait.

Close seasons:

Red deer (Cervus elaphus)
Stags 1st May to 31st July incl.
Hinds Ist March to 31st October incl.

Fallow deer (Dam dama)
Buck 1st May to 31st July incl.
Doe Ist March to 31st October incl

Roe deer (Capreolus capreolus)
Buck Ist November to 31st March incl.
Doe Ist March to 31st October incl.

Sica deer (Cervus nippon)
Stags Ist May to 31st July incl.
Hinds Ist March to 31st October incl.

The Venison Dinner Committee

During recent years the Committee has consisted of representatives from local voluntary organisations, commerce, the local authorities and the local council.

The medallion depicted on the cover is worn by members when attending the dinner.

The present Committee:

President	Sir Ray Tindle.
Chairman	Mr Frank Cordier.
	Dame Elizabeth Anson.
	Mr Robert Cozens
	Mr Frederick Culver.
	Mrs Pamela Frost
	Mr Anthony Geary
	Mrs Anne Hoath
	Mr Harry Lawrence
	Mr Donald Scott
	Mrs Pamela Woodroffe.
	The Town Mayor and Town Clerk
	Farnham Town Council - Ex Officio

Bibliography and Acknowledgements

Newspaper archives:
Andover Advertiser
Farnham Herald
Hampshire Chronicle
Surrey Advertiser
Surrey Comet
Surrey & Hants News

Books/Articles/Minutes:
A Victorian History of Surrey. University of London
British Borough Charters
Church and Parish. J.H.Batty
Crockford's Clerical Directory. 1998/99
Edward Harold Browne. A Memoir. Rev. G.W.Kitchen
English History Documents. 1783-1832. D.C.Douglas
Farnham and Its Borough. 1859. Rev. R.N.Milford
Farnham and its Surroundings. Gordon Home
Farnham Bailiff's Accounts and Court Books
Farnham Buildings and People. Nigel Temple
Farnham Inheritance. N.H.L.Temple
Farnham Town Walk. 1975. Waverley D.C.
Farnham Souvenir. W.Chapman.
Hampshire Record Office. References: 11M59/E2/153269, 11M59/E2/153270, 11M59/E2/155545, 44M69/J31/4
History of Farnham. 1925. W.L.White and H.R.Huband
Hops and Hop Picking. Richard Filmer
Kelly's Directory 1887.
Life and Customs in Gilbert Whites' Cobbett's and Kingsley's County.
    J Alfred Eggar
Life of Charles Richard Sumner. G.H.Sumner
Lloyds Bank archives.
Medieval Farnham. E.Robbo
Minutes of the Vestry, Local Board, Farnham U.D.C.,
    Waverley BC, Farnham Consultative Committee, Farnham Town Council
Petition of Farnham U.D.C., 1925
Reminiscences of a Country Town. John Henry Knight.
Surrey History Service. Reference 1505/-

The Brewers Almanac 1971
The Episcopal Palaces of England. Precentor Venables
The Mild Prosperity of Farnham. Winifred Newman.
The Surrey Magazine. 1900
The Village Labourer. J.L. & B. Hammond
Tour through the Whole Island. Daniel de Foe.
Weyhill Fair. Anthony C.Raper
Whigs and Hunters.E.P.Thompson
Whitakers Almanac 1888
Winchester Cathedral Record. 1996

Acknowledgment is made of the helpful assistance given by the Archivists and staff of the following establishments:
Army museum, Clandon Park.
Highclere Castle, Near Newbury
Surrey History Centre, Woking
The Museum of Farnham
Winchester Local Studies Office
Winchester Record Offices

In particular acknowledgement is made of the kind permissions granted by the following to reproduce photographs and documents:
The Earl of Carnarvon
Sir Ray Tindle
Episcopalian Bishop of Maryland America.
Country Life
Mrs Florence Alum
Mrs Jean Parratt
Mr Chris Shepheard

The author, Fred Culver, is grateful to Tindle Newspapers for their assistance with the preparation and printing of this book.

INDEX

A
Abbotts Hosp: 75
Aberfan: 83
Addy, L: 87
Ald & Dist.Emp.Cttee: 77
Ald. Military Camp: 42
Aldridge: 68
Almshouses, Windsor: 31
Andernach: 92,95
Anderson, R.D: 68
Anderson, Mrs R: 75
Andrews, F: 43
Andrews, S: 36
Anson, Lady E: 88
Archbishop, Cantab: 52,60
" York: 81
Artizens Dwellings Act: 53
Atkins: 70, 72.
Aubrey: 31
Aylett: 86,87
Aylott: 41
Aylwin: 43,53

B
Bailiffs:
" Bookham, J: 13
" Bicknell: 19
" Clark, J: 11
" Grene, W: 13
" Piggott: 16
" Searle: 16
" Terrye, W: 13
" Tomson, R: 13
" Warner, R: 13
" Wroth, H: 13
" Wroth, N: 19.
" Accounts:12,17,18,20, 21,23,26
" Book: 13
" Feasts: 7,13,19,27,28
" Salaries: 20
Banks:
" Capital & Counties: 33
" James Knight: 33
" Lloyds: 33
" Stevens: 33
Bacon, Capt: 61
Baker: 70
Ballard: 41.
Bateman, J.F: 42
Barrett, R.T: 43,47.
Baxter,G: 77
Beale, R: 43,46,53
Beaver, T: 61
Bentall, J: 43,57
Bide, S: 57
Birch, F.C: 43
Birch, W: 35
Bishops:
" Adie, M.E: 88,93
" Andrews, L:75
" Bilson, T: 12,15
" Browne, D: 87
" Browne, E.H: 51
" Curll, W: 16
" Davidson, R: 58,60
" of Dorking:94
" Duppa, B: 6,20
" Episcopalian: 7
" Evans, K.D: 87
" Gardiner, S: 20
" Greig, J.H: 77
" of Guildford: 75,94
" Hoadley, B:26
" Horne, R:7,11,28
" MacMillan, J.V:79
" Mews, P: 24
" Montgomery-Campbell, H.C:79
" Morley, R: 20,22,24,35,68,88
" North.B: 24,29,31,32,56,61,65,96
" Ponet, J: 20
" Reindorp, G.E: 82
" Ryle, E.H: 60,63,64,65,67,68
" St.Swithuns: 5
" Sumner, C:34,35,41,49,50,51,77,90

" Talbot, E.S: 68,71,72,73
" Thomas, J: 30,31
" Thorold, A.W: 56
" Trelawney, J: 24,25,30
" Trimnell, C: 30
" Watkins. I: 82
" White, J: 7
" Wilcox, D: 93
" Wilberforce, S: 49,50
" Wilfred: 5
" Woods, F.T: 74,75
Bishop's Cage:11,29
Bishops Waltham: 16
Black Act: 25
Blissimere Hall: 33
Blois, Henry de: 68
Blohn, G.von: 95
Board for Highways: 37
Bolton: 72
Bone, H: 26
Bonnard: 68
Borelli.C:57,67,68,72,74,75,76,80,94
" Cup: 76
" Grapes: 89
Borough Rent:ll
Bowler: 43
Bransby-Williams Lt.Col.M: 92
Braybent , J: 17
Breil, Herr F:95
Brewer, Capt: 19
Bridge,Tilford: 6.28
Bridgeland: 28
Bristow, A: 27,28
Brittain, Sir H:80
Brodrick, Hat: 60`
" Rt.Hon.St, J: 59,60,72
Bromley,E: 42,43,45,46,49,53
Brown, Dr: 57
Browne.Rev.B.G: 52
Brumwell.G: 73
Bryant: 43
Bubb, T.H: 57
Bullers, Sir R: 58
Burch: 53
Burial Board: 36

Bush Hotel:12,13,32,41,42,46,47,49,
53,56,57,61,62,67,74,75,77,79
Butchers' Shambles: 23.
By-Pass: 78,79,81,
Byworth Cup:14,65,68,73,81,94,95
" J: 14.
" Sermon: 14.

C

Caldman: 43
Chandler, K.T: 84,86,87
Chapman, A.W: 58,60
Charter:
" 688: 5
" 839: 5
" 858: 5
" 909: 6
" 1248: 6
" 1266: 6
" 1410: 6,20
" 1566: 7,11,22,23
" Book of: 6
" Town: 81
Christmas Gift Fund: 72
Civic Sunday: 14
Civil War:15,16,17,18
Clapham, John: 19
Clapham, Joshua: 19
Clark.E.Caterers: 84,87
Clark, Judge G: 81
Clark G,: 36
Clayton,Rev.T: 69
Cobbett,Silver Cup: 84
Cobbett, W: 34,77
Coleman: 57,61
Collyer: 35
Combe, R.H: 54,76
Cordier, R.F: 86,87,90,91
Corn Exchange:41,59,62,63,68,71,73
Court Book: 11
" Meeting: 11,13
" Leet: 29,49,74
" Baron: 29,49,74
Coyne, D: 84
Cowan, W.H: 63,64

Cromwell, O: 17,18,20,74
Crook:43,45
Crooksbury, Firs: 26
Crum, J.M.C: 71
Crump, W: 36
Crundwell, E: 57,58
Cubitt.51,52
Culver Hall: 18
Cumberland Friendly Soc: 31

D
Darvill, J: 54
Deer: 14,15,16,31,72,74
   " Leap: 15
DeFoe, D: 27
Drake-Wilkes, P:94.
Drinkwater, R: 36
Duty, Beer: 32

E
Ealand, Dr: 68,74
Ecclesiastical:
    " Leasing Act: 41
    " Commission: 49,74,76,90
Ede,C:77
Edwards, D: 43
Eggar, J.A: 57,62,63,65,68,70
Ellicott, B: 16
Ellis: 49
Elphick, G: 57
Employ. of Labourers: 37
Emery, W.H: 79
Evans, S: 76
Ewart, W: 74
Eyre, T: 36,43

F
Fair, Sunday: 6
Fairs: 6,11,22
Fairfax, T: 17
Falcard: 68
Falkner, H: 41

Farnham Am. Operatic Soc.: 83
   " & County Hop Planters: 54
   " & Dist.War Relief Fund: 71 "
   Castle: 12,13,15,16,17,19, 20,22,25,27,30,34,49,51, 52,60,67,73,74,75,77,79, 83,87,88,93,94
   " Gas Co: 35,59
   " Jr. Childrens' Choir: 81
   " Land & Bldg Soc: 31
   " Mkt. House & Town
   " Hall Co. Ltd: 41
   " Farnham, Parks: 14,15,16,24,25,30,32,56, 69,72,74,76,77,78,84
   " Presbyterianism: 19
   " Town Plan 1947: 91
   " United Breweries: 64
Farwell, J: 20
Fenn Messrs: 64
Ferguson: 72
Figg, A.J: 68,72,75
Finbows: 88
Fish Cross: 23
Fisher: 67
Fitzpatrick, Sir. P: 70
Forbes, E: 24
Foster: 49
Foster, Maj.H: 76
French, Gen.Sir J: 60
Friendly Socs. Act: 53
Fry: 57
Fuchs, Herr & Frau: 95

G
Gardiner, Rev.T.G: 57
George,Lloyd: 77
German: 68
Gilbert,Sen: 43
Gilbert, H: 43
Gill,T.H: 24
Gilpin, W: 27
Ginger: 45
Goats Head P.H: 7,31,41

Goddard, D: 53,57
Gold, J: 20
Goldsmith, 0: 81
Goodman: 49
Goodman, Lord: 83
Goodwyn, G: 17
Goujon: 53
Gould, C: 57
Gosport Dil. Stagecoach: 31
Gostrey Meadow: 68,71
Granville, Lord: 50
Gray, H.G: 35
Gregory.J: 47
Grenville-Grey, W.E: 87
Guildford Cath: 79,82

H

Hackman: 43
Haddington, Lord: 12,15
Hale, Chief Baron: 22
Hammond: 49
Hampton Ct. Palace: 18
Harding: 13
Hart, F: 57
Hay, W: 31
Hayes, Dr: 57
Heath, G: 57
Henriques, Sir P: 78
Heron, Steward: 24
Hewitt: 53
Hicks-Baach, Sir M: 60
Highways: 30
Hilary Folk: 87
Hillkirk, Maj: 57,58
Hoare,T: 43
Hoaste,Rev.P: 52
Hoath Mrs A: 87,90
Hodgson: 43
Holland, Earl of: 17
Holland, E.J: 76
Hollest, J: 29
Holtzappffell: 43,44
Hook, C: 35
Hook & Frost: 29.

Hop, Duty: 26,32,37,40,42
" Betting:37,38,39,42,51,52, 57,61
" Costs: 40,47,63
" Crop: 38,54,57
" Fairs: 36
" Grounds: 23,27,31,49
" Kent: 41,49,63
" Prices: 34,35,36,47
" Sunday: 34
Horne, Rev. C . J: 36
Hurdle, A: 84,85,86,87,88
Hütton, Herr A: 95

I

Insp. Lighting & Watch: 35
Isolation Hosp: 58

J

Jackson, E: 61,71
James, Col: 16
James,W: 47
Jarrow: 78
Jarvis,Sir J: 78
Johnson: 43,46
Jones, H: 79
Jones: 72
Joynes, Mrs M: 81

K

Kemp: 61
Kempson, N.E: 57,67,68
Keney, Mary: 47
Kent, K: 91
Kersie: 14
Kessell: 65
Kime,K: 84
King, Aethelbond: 5
" Caedwalla: 5
" Charles 1: 7,15,18
" Charles 11: 32,74
" Edward V1: 20
" George 111: 29
" James 1: 12,13,14,75
" John: 6.

" George V:70
" Harold V: 70.
" Henry VII: 68
Kilvert, T: 20,21
Kimber, Mrs K: 77
Kingham, D: 57,58,68
"King John": 25
Kirby, Woodward:24
Knights Folly: 33
Knight, G.C: 29
" G.V: 43
" James: 41,42,47,50,52
" James, jnr: 43
" J.C:36,37,53
Klinkhammer, Dr: 92
Kuschev: 82

L
Lancet, The: 48
Lancaster, H.H: 84,87
Larby, E: 25
Lawday Hse.Common: 35
Lawrence, H: 86,90.
Leadenhall Mkt: 68
Leefe, Gen: 64
Legge, R: 18
Lighting & Watch: 48
Lindsay: 43,45
Lion & Lamb Inn: 35,37
Local Board: 44,45,71
Local Gov. Act 1858: 46
" 1888: 56
" 1894: 56
" 1972: 84
Lock, J: 57
Lorimer: 50
Lorrimer, Dr: 57
Lord Mayor, London: 7
Lord of the Manor: 20,29,75,90
Lowndes: 43
Lucy, A.E: 43,44
Lucy, A.K: 46
Lunn, Mary: 30,31

M
Maberley: 21
MacMillan, Rt.Hon. M: 87
Maillard, Col: 57,58
Mainwaring, J: 29
Manning, Mrs O: 84
Mardon, A.G: 65,67.72.74,76
Maltings: 88
Market, Corn: 14,19,23,24,25,26,29
" Cloth: 14,19
" House: 11,12,17,21,29,39, 41
" Wheat: 14,19,23,25,27
Mason, A.E: 57
Mason, R: 47
Mason, W: 36
Masters & Workman's Act: 53
Mathews: 53
May, P.B.H: 82
Mayen-Koblenz: 91
Mayges, G: 93
Memorial Hall: 80,81,88
Menu: 43,53,54,67,76,84
McCutcheon, E: 43
McCutcheon, J: 43
Michaux: 43
Midleton,Lord: 60,72,73,74,77,78
Militia: 30,44
Miller, G: 36
Mitchell, H: 65,68
Mompesson, Sir G: 13
Montgomery, Field Marshall Viscount: 82
Montgomery, Viscount: 91
Moody: 45,50,53
Moore, Sir G: 15
Morgan, F.A: 76,77,80
Morning Cap: 18
Mosier, J: 21
Museum: 78

N
Nash, J: 43,46,53
Nationwide Bldg Soc: 24
Newland, C: 21

Newnham, N: 36
Nichols, H: 36
Nichols, J. Jnr: 43,53
Nobody's Friends Hotel: 56
Non ulterius presequi: 20

O
O'Connell, D: 77
Old Bull & Crown: 78
Old Goats Head P.H: 7,31,41
Overseas Service: 82
Oulton: 30
Open Spaces Act 1906: 77.

P
Paine, W.P: 36
Parish Church, Seats: 12
Peerman, A: 69
Peperharow Park: 69,72
Percival, F: 43,44,45,46
Petition:
" Charter of Incorp: 71
" Further Privileges: 18
" Lighting & Watch: 36
" Local Board: 57
" London Mers: 54
" Road Protest: 48,49
" Railway: 54,58,59
Piggott: 19
Political Reg. 1831: 43
Poor, Guardians: 48
Poor Law Act 1601: 31
" Overseers:
" Eyre, T: 31
" Trimmer, R: 31
Poperinge: 69
Portsmouth, Earl of: 7
Potter, H: 43,45
Powell, Lord B: 78
Powell: 31
Presbyterianism: 19
Preston: 68
Priestland, B: 75
Priestley, Rev. S: 57
Price: 64

Private Encl. Act: 25
Public Address Sys: 84

Q
Queen, Elizabeth 1: 7,28,47
"   "   11: 70
"   Victoria: 42.
Quo Warranto: 21

R
Radcliffe-Maude, Comm: 84
Raggett: 43
Railway: 48,54,58,59,63,78
Ransom: 57
Ranson: 74
Ranson & Sons: 63
Rates, Church: 37
" Lighting & Watch: 37
" Poor: 30,31,37
" Rep. Highways: 37
Rathmall, Mrs: 87
Redgrave Theatre: 83
Reed, J: 37
Rifle Volunteers: 53
Roberts, G: 61
Rope Walk: 26
Ross, J: 81
Royal Warrant: 7
Roydon, M: 21,22

S
Samson R: 63
Samuel: 74,75,77
Scott, D: 89
Scribban, V: 87
Seale of Town: 11
Sellers, J: 69
Shah of Persia: 50
Shaw, N: 33
Shephard, Dr: 50
Shotter, J: 36
Shotter, W: 27,28,29,65
Shurlock, R: 36
Simmonds, A: 57
Smallman, Brig. A: 90

Smith, Capt: 76
Smith, PC: 47
Smith, T: 43
Snowden, Lady: 79
Soup kitchen: 54
Southern, Rev. E. G: 79
Speak, F.W: 67
Steere, L: 51,52,53
Stevens, A: 74,77
Stevens, J: 33,36,37
St. James Church: 51
Stone, D: 93
Stourbridge Fair: 32
Streets, Condition of: 18
Sturgeons: 15,20
Stroud, Mrs: 74,79,88
Sumner, Rev.J: 50,51
Surrey Police: 47
Swanborough: 70,71

T
Talbot, G: 69
Talbot, Hon. Mrs: 73
Talbot, N: 69
Tanner, Dr: 68
Taylor, N: 93
Thursday lecture: 16
Tice, A: 77
Tichbourne, J: 16
Tigwell: 67
Tiley, W: 57
Tindle, Sir R: 96
Toc H: 69
Town Hall: 35,41,42,43,44,47,54,57,60
Town Feast: 12,13,15,17,18,19,20,21,24.
Tradesman's Dinner: 47
Transvaal: 57
Treasurer's House: 36
Treacher, Sir W.H: 63
Trimmer, G: 36,54
Trimmer, R.G: 57
Trinada necessitas: 5
Tuck, Rev.A: 93
Two minute silence: 70

U
Unemployment Fund: 71
User, Col: 18

V
Varndall, R: 43
Vaughan, W: 35
Venison Dinner, Andover: 7
   "   "   Cttee: 30,37,53,56,
   "   "   62,68,69,70,72,80,
   "   "   84,86,87,90,92,93,
             94,96
   "   "   Kingston: 7
Venison Dinner, Tickets: 68,75,79,80,84,87, 92,94
Venison, Distribution: 56,69
Venison Feast, Cost: 15,17,32
Vernon House: 18
Vestry: 27
Vine: 43,53

W
Wainwright, J: 91
Waltham Blacks: 25
Waltham Forest: 25,26
Watchmen, Beagley, W: 36
   "   Cole,T: 36
   "   Steere,J: 36
Water Co: 35
Water supply: 24
Watkins, Mrs: 73
Waverley, Abbey: 81
   "   B.C: 84,86,91,95
   "   School: 42
Weller, Capt. R: 16
Weller, Sir W: 16,17
Weyhill Fair: 32,33,34,47,54,57,63
White, P: 92
Wilds, Cannon H: 94
Williams: 57
Williams, J.R: 36
Will, Black: 26
Wilton, Dr: 42

Windsor, A: 87
Winter, A.W: 54
Wither, Capt G: 16
Woodbine: 53
Woodbourne: 43
Workhouse: 30,31,48,61
Ward, Maj.O: 53
Wright, J.W: 65,67,68

Y
Young, G: 35
Young, Mrs: 39
Young, R: 35